C000070317

TAMING THE BEAST

JOHN FLETCHER SMYTH
MA, MB, BChir, MD.(Cantab), MSc (Lond), FRCPE, FRC
FRCSE, FRCR, FRSE, FACP(UK)

Emeritus Professor of Medical Oncology
University of Edinburgh

TAMING

THE

BEAST

Memoirs *of a*
Pioneering Cancer Physician

JOHN F. SMYTH

Maclean Dubois

This edition first published in hardback in Great Britain in
2022 by Maclean Dubois
14/2 Gloucester Place, Edinburgh EH3 6EF

ISBN: 978-0-9565278-1-3

Copyright © John F. Smyth, 2022

All rights reserved. No part of this publication may
be reproduced, stored, or transmitted in any form, or
by any means electronic, mechanical or photocopying,
recording or otherwise, without the express written
permission of the publisher.

The moral right of John F. Smyth to be identified as the
author of this work has been asserted by him in accordance
with the Copyright, Designs and Patents Act 1988.

British Library Cataloguing-in-Publication Data
A catalogue record for this book is available on request
from the British Library.

Designed and typeset by Abigail Salvesen.
Printed and bound by Gutenberg Press Ltd, Malta.

For Ann

FOREWORD

It is a truism that bears repeating: everybody has a story that is worth telling. Or almost everybody: there must be some lives that never quite reach the bar that is needed to maintain our interest. But they are few, I suspect. They are at one end of the spectrum of memoirs: at the other end, there are biographies and autobiographies with which we engage on page one and remain riveted to for every page that follows, right up to the end. These tell of lives that have been full of interest and incident and may even have changed the world for the better. This memoir by John Smyth is one of those.

What is particularly striking about this account of a life lived through the second half of the last century and into the present day, is the range of the interests that have sustained the author. Prominent amongst these is music, in which he had the great advantage in life of having a choral training. Making music with others is not only a great pleasure for those involved, but stands as a metaphor for the ability to co-operate that we need if we are to achieve anything very much. Those who keep to themselves, who plough a lonely furrow, may get somewhere in life, but they are far less likely to achieve anything than those who are ready to work with others. John Smyth's musical career brought him into contact with musicians of considerable stature and gave him something that lasted him a lifetime. Which, of course, is what music does: it stays with us, sustains us, makes sense of a world that can at times be testing and confusing. But more than that, music humanises.

And that has an important bearing on the professional career that John pursued and that provides the main pillar of this fascinating book. Those with a sufficiently long memory will recall the time when there was little that medicine could do for those afflicted by cancer. That was the dread disease, spoken of in hushed tones, often concealed from the patient himself or herself. A diagnosis of cancer was, in fairly recent times, a terminal diagnosis. I remember talking to a paediatric oncologist friend who said that at the start of his career his job was a bleak one indeed – there was very little he could do. Then, with the development of a whole range of new drugs, he was suddenly able to offer hope. Now he went in to work each day knowing that there was at last something he could do for the children in his care.

Each of the new drugs in his armamentarium, of course, was the result of a long and complicated process of research. Penicillin may have grown by chance in a petri dish on a lab window, but that is not how these powerful cancer drugs are discovered today. Long years of enquiry, observation, and painstaking testing lie in the hinterland of such medicines, and behind all that work there stand people who have been prepared to devote their lives to the task of conquering disease. Their story can be a fascinating one, combining long periods of hard slog with moments of insight and breakthrough. It is one of the most exciting detective stories there is, with, in so many cases, a happy ending.

In this wonderful account of his life as a pioneering oncologist, we are given the story of a life spent in that important and edifying work. The author is modest throughout, but those writing a foreword need not be so constrained. John Smyth's contribution to the treatment of cancer has been very significant. This is not the account of a bystander – it is the story of a frontline combatant.

Scottish medicine has had many heroes in the past. This is the story of one of them. But it is also the story of a man who has made music with others, who can fly an aeroplane, who has made many friendships, and to whom there are many who, quite simply, owe their lives. So any foreword to a story of that nature should end, it seems to me, with two words: thank you.

ALEXANDER McCALL SMITH

CONTENTS

20 November, 1978: The day that changed my life

I had been interviewed for jobs before, but it had never been anything like this. Usually, there would be about half a dozen people on the panel. Here there were twenty.

Then again, this was no ordinary interview. Edinburgh University was about to decide who should be its first professor of medical oncology. And in November 1978, when I was shown into the large room in Old College to face an eighty-minute inquisition by the great and the good of Scotland's finest medical school and Britain's best cancer physicians, the subject was of more than academic interest. Scotland's cancer rates were the highest in the world, having almost doubled over the previous half century.

There was another reason why the five candidates faced such a crowded interviewing panel. Unlike most academic subjects, medical oncology was to be established in Edinburgh with particularly generous funding. In the 1970s, cancer research in Britain was led by charities funding academic chairs in medical oncology in the hope that this would lead to the development of new drugs for the wide range of cancers for which there was still no effective treatment. The funding being provided by the Imperial Cancer Research Fund (ICRF) for the new Edinburgh chair was in fact far beyond anything offered anywhere else in the country. Better still, its £800,000 was to be matched by Lothian NHS in funding for doctors, nurses and beds. Whoever got the job wouldn't have to face the time-consuming battles for staff and resources that could bedevil similar projects elsewhere.

Of the twenty people in front of me, there were

two in particular I knew I would have to impress. Sir Eric Scowan, a revered professor of medicine at Barts in London who looked remarkably like Alfred Hitchcock, had chaired the ICRF council for years. The Edinburgh project was close to his heart, as it represented the charity's first major investment outside London. His friendship with Edinburgh University's principal, Sir Hugh Robson, was one of the reasons they had decided to set up the chair at the city's Western General Hospital, though the high reputation of the university's four hundred-year-old medical school and of the hospital's radiotherapy and surgery would have also weighed heavily in Edinburgh's favour. Robson had died unexpectedly a year before this interview and so the chair was taken by the university's acting principal, Professor Berrick Saul. He was seated opposite me behind a huge table, with Sir Eric on his right and the dean of medicine on his left. The rest – representing surgery, medicine, radiotherapy, haematology, pathology, the Medical Research Council, Lothian Health Board and the university – were sitting at tables on either side. Facing them all, I tried hard not to feel intimidated.

What would they make of me? I wasn't Scottish, hadn't studied at Edinburgh or worked even briefly at any of the city's hospitals. I was also only thirty-three. Wasn't that ridiculously young for a professorship? And what about that rumour that the job I was *really* interested in was the chair in medical oncology at the Royal Marsden, where I had spent the last two years as a senior lecturer?

They all had copies of my CV in front of them, and the basics of my medical training were all there: Cambridge, Barts, and my work there with Gordon Hamilton Fairley, the charismatic founding father of British oncology who had been killed by an IRA bomb four years previously. They knew, too, about my research work in the States, and how deoxycoformycin (DCF) – my main claim to fame in cancer circles – was proving an effective drug for treating acute lymphocytic leukaemia and other lymphoid malignancies. I didn't want to ruin my chances by appearing immodest, but I knew that I had probably had the best training in medical oncology of anyone in the UK at that time, and I had a clear idea of how the specialty could develop.

There were only four professors of medical oncology in Britain at that time and two of them were on the panel as external assessors. I knew that they would understand and appreciate my work on DCF, but convincing the rest that I was the right person to set up and lead an entire department when I had never done anything like it, and overcoming any reluctance to appoint the youngest professor of medical oncology in the country, required more than that. They wanted, presumably, to reassure themselves that I had the wide interests and people skills necessary for the job.

Here, I thought, I could potentially score. There is, and always has been, more to me than medicine. Ever since university, I have loved flying. Ever since school, I have adored choral singing – and at a high level too: the Monteverdi Choir, with which I have sung for fifty years, is often praised as one of the best in the world. And I seriously doubted whether any of the other candidates would be able to match my own record of having helped deliver a baby, flown a Tiger Moth and recorded a classical CD – all in the same day!

Yet my interview got off to a terrible start. When Prof Saul, presumably trying to calm my nerves, asked me if I'd miss singing in the Monteverdi Choir if I did get the job in Edinburgh, I replied that I'd still hope to be part of it, and it wouldn't matter too much as they had very few rehearsals. I could have kicked myself. I had gone into the interview determined that whatever happened, I wouldn't let myself down, yet that was exactly what I'd just done. Everyone in the room was looking for a candidate who would devote *all* their energies to the new task in Edinburgh, and yet I'd just implied that I'd be dashing off to London whenever the Monteverdi wanted me. I tried to recover by mentioning my friendship with Herrick Bunney, the university's organist and master of music at St Giles' Cathedral, adding that I hoped to sing in the cathedral choir too.

I hoped it was enough to convince them, because the preliminary soundings I had taken in Edinburgh revealed a lot of support for me from other specialists. Even though I realised that some of this might be because they thought the new professorship could be a potential source of funding for their own collaborative projects, I was greatly encouraged. If I did go for the chair at the Royal Marsden – for which I was under consideration – I knew I would have my work cut out dealing with the resentment and rivalries of my colleagues. In Edinburgh, I sensed, I would be free of that.

And then there was the sheer challenge of the job, of building something from nothing. Its demands were twofold: first, spreading the word about what medical oncology could offer within the NHS and establishing Edinburgh as a place for cancer research; secondly, within the university, leading collaborative research projects and teaching the subject at both undergraduate and – later – postgraduate level. The interview panel (in those distant and less enlightened days, all men) asked a series of penetrating questions about how I would expect to do all of this, and what kind of leader I would be. Each of the panellists asked a question, taking it in turn clockwise round the room, with several coming back for a second one.

How on earth, someone asked, would I find the time to do such a demanding job as well as continuing to sing in choirs and pilot light aircraft? That was easy to answer. Cancer, I pointed out, inevitably took a toll on those who treated it. Physicians needed to ensure that they weren't ground down by repeatedly failing to bring about either remission or cure, and both singing and flying could provide a necessary release. Paradoxically, flying is particularly good in this respect as it demands intense concentration – you are, after all, taking your life in your hands on every take-off and landing. Besides which, I added, didn't it all just go to show that I was quite good at time management?

Towards the end of the interview, Sir Eric Scowan asked the key question. 'Well, Smyth,' he said. 'If you were to be offered this post in Edinburgh, it might be that the Royal Marsden would decide to offer you their chair instead. In that case, what would be your response?'

Without a moment's hesitation, I replied: 'Well sir, in that event I would consider myself a very fortunate young man!' This brought the house down.

Of course, I then answered that if I was privileged enough to be offered the post in Edinburgh, I would accept it, and that I was absolutely not attending this interview merely to increase my chances of getting the chair at the Royal Marsden.

Later that afternoon, I was asked to telephone Prof Saul. He offered me Edinburgh's first chair of medical oncology. My life would never be the same again.

TAMING THE BEAST

PROLOGUE

I have led an interesting and varied life and from time to time have wondered whether I should write about it and, if I did, whether anyone would be interested, or whether my autobiography's only use would be to enable me to count my blessings in a more orderly fashion. Nothing has ever mattered to me more than family, and one stimulus for writing this was the affectionate curiosity about my life from several of my six grandchildren and four step-grandchildren. There have been many occasions when they have asked 'Have you ever done this, or ever been to. . .?' So maybe one day, if they ever read this, they will find out more than they knew about 'Grandpa John' and be amused. But I hope that other readers will be interested in my recounting some of the extraordinary progress that has been made in the management of cancer over the past fifty years, as we have sought to 'tame' many of the common malignant diseases.

Not many people have the opportunity or challenge of being a professor of medicine for thirty years and in this book I will try to summarise some of the highlights of creating the specialty of medical oncology in Scotland and establishing the Edinburgh Cancer Research Centre, now recognised as one of the foremost of its kind in Europe. As one of its pioneers, I have spent a lot of my professional life helping to develop oncology in Europe, and am proud to have been the only British person ever President of the European Society of Medical Oncology. I am saddened by the decision of the UK to leave the European Union, and I doubt whether any other British oncologist will be honoured in this way in the future.

While I was at Cambridge I learnt to fly in the RAF. I have continued flying as a private pilot ever since and have recollected some of my flying adventures here. The skills and discipline necessary for flying – especially if you are on your own – have informed several other aspects of my life, and I like to think that it keeps me young. Music has also been hugely important to me, and in parallel with my life in medicine, I have sung at a professional level for more than fifty years.

I decided not to write in detail about other family and friends to avoid intrusion into privacy, but I devote a short chapter to the late Bishop Launcelot Fleming, who played a pivotal role in my youth, especially in helping me to decide to accept the offer of the chair in Edinburgh. I still miss his wise counsel. I also pay tribute to my wife Ann, my closest friend and, in her own words, 'fiercest critic'. She knows me better than anyone else ever has, and her tolerance is a source of constant surprise to me – and probably most of our friends!

In trying to summarise a long life as an academic physician, I have focused on some of the major landmarks that illustrate our progress in taming the many different diseases that we now recognise under the umbrella of 'cancer'. When I started my career in cancer medicine back in the 1970s, we had so few tools to work with. Diagnosis was almost exclusively dependent on the pathologist looking down a microscope; we only had basic X-rays to establish the extent of disease and didn't have CT scans, let alone MRI or PET. Surgery and radiotherapy were well established but we had very few medicines and all forms of treatment incurred significant side-effects. While we dreamed that one day we might cure cancer, we realised that the first steps must be to find ways to slow the progression of the disease – to tame the wild beast of malignancy and help patients to live with their cancer in the same way that people have to live with chronic diseases such as diabetes, hypertension, and arthritis. Thanks to the efforts of doctors and scientists and the cooperation of thousands of patients worldwide, we have now succeeded in taming many of the common cancers. Of course, there is still so much to do, but in this memoir I will summarise some of the highlights of my own contribution to this exciting story.

In 530 BC the Athenian poet Solon wrote, 'Call no man happy before he dies; he is at best but fortunate.' I disagree. I recognise how fortunate I have been, but I am also happy – and grateful.

1. EARLY DAYS

The patch of the planet that meant the most to my family last century is a small bit of southern Gloucestershire halfway between Bristol and Gloucester. My father was born in Sharpness, a port on the Severn Estuary, where the large tidal range makes it ideal for ships to enter for repairs. I was born five miles inland, in the small town of Dursley. My father was the works manager of RA Lister & Co, its main employer, a heavy engineering company that switched from making agricultural tools and diesel engines to producing aeroplanes, spares for aircraft and shell casings during the Second World War. Because of his job, he was not allowed to join the armed forces. Most of his friends did volunteer, many of them died, and I think that this difference had a significant effect on his later life.

I was born on 26 October 1945 in my parents' bedroom at The Rise, on Woodland Drive, a quiet cul de sac with views west to the Welsh hills. We lived there until the autumn of 1948, although apart from one night when a chimney caught fire and my brother Robert and I were lifted from our beds amid the noise and excitement of an arriving fire engine, I have no memories of the place. I have a few more of the next place we lived – 225 Fox

Lane, Southgate, in North London – a semi-detached house on a busy main road, but with a small garden at the back. My mother hated it, but I fondly remember the big chestnut tree I could see from our bedroom (my brother Robert, a year older, shared a room with me until we were late teenagers) and a sandpit where I played with my friends. As was the case those days with most married women with children, my mother did not go out to work. Instead, she kept house and looked after Robert and me.

My father had moved us there following the offer of a job from my godfather, after whom I am named – John Panchaud. I will write more about him later, since he had a big influence on all our lives. Father worked for an engineering company, Dysons of Enfield, then ran a timber mill in Uxbridge, before finally joining John and his brother Gerald Panchaud, who were directors of a company called Harlow & Jones. The Panchauds were true entrepreneurs and in the post-war years demonstrated great skill and enterprise in spotting commercial opportunities. The biggest project Harlow & Jones undertook in the early post-war years was working as scrap metal merchants in the Netherlands, Belgium and northern France, which were then still littered with the detritus of war – tanks, lorries, guns, crashed aeroplanes and the like. No-one wanted these horrid reminders of war, and they were an obstacle to rehabilitating the land. The Panchauds offered to collect them, bought a smelting plant in Rotterdam and, at no cost to anyone else, cleared the debris and smelted it down to extract zinc. As there was a worldwide shortage of the metal at the time, they made a fortune.

Age seven with my brother Robert, who was one year older.
We were very close throughout our childhood.

Roselands, the house where I grew up in Beaconsfield.

Exactly what part my father played in all this I do not know. Almost certainly, the business plan and strategy came from the Panchauds, but father was always good with people and at project management. When he became a director of Harlow & Jones, his office moved to one of the more prestigious addresses in central London –18 Buckingham Gate, a stone's throw from Buckingham Palace. My parents could now afford to buy a family house, and in deciding where to live within commuting distance of his new office, they gave education for Robert and me top priority.

Of all the things that my parents did for me, I am especially grateful for their concern for our schooling. Both of them had left school at the age of fourteen and had no higher education. However, they clearly appreciated the value of a good preparatory school. When they found Davenies Boys Preparatory School in Beaconsfield, they decided to buy Roselands, a large, mock-Tudor 1930s detached house in Beechwood Road, just a short cycle ride away. Both were excellent choices.

We moved to Beaconsfield in 1952 when I was seven and stayed until I was eighteen. Roselands had an oak-panelled dining room with an open fireplace, and there was a music room to house Robert's Blüthner grand piano. My parents cleared a rose garden to create a large lawn on which we practised cricket, and there was an orchard with thirty or so apple trees whose produce was stored in a concrete air-raid shelter left over from the war. For the first few years, I was very happy there. My father used to say that the Chiltern Hills in Buckinghamshire reminded both him and my mother of the Cotswolds, but by the time we moved to Roselands my parents' lives had changed almost beyond recognition from the early days in and around Dursley. Let me record some of what I know about their early lives, and their family origins.

My father was christened Henry James Robert Smyth (1909-1979), but always known as Bob. His father, Robert Smyth (1869-1932) was a merchant sea captain, about whom I know little other than that he was born in Carrickfergus, lived at Sharpness and died in Dursley and that his mother was born in Scotland, so I have inherited Irish, English and Scottish ancestry. I do not think my father knew grandfather very well: as a sea captain, grandfather Robert was away for long periods of time, and when he returned from the sea, he suffered from severe Parkinson's disease, which can make people seem remote and possibly frightening to the young.

Grandfather Robert was a religious man – as many seafarers were – and used to write devout and devoted letters from distant parts to his wife Alice. He made repeated voyages round the Cape of Good Hope to India and the Far East, where he visited Shanghai. When I went there for the first time and walked along the Bund, I thought of him and the relative frailty of the ships that would have taken him there and all the dangers he would have faced.

Robert's wife Alice (1883-1935) had a hard life, bringing up my father and his older sister Eileen single-handed when Robert was away at sea, and then dying of a stroke at the young age of fifty-two. She is buried with him in the cemetery at Saint Mark's church, Dursley. Under the headstone is carved 'After she hath striven', which I find both strange and sad. She was, however, helped by her father, Henry Atkins, who lived with them and was the most important and influential person in my father's youth. He too was a merchant seaman, but after a serious accident which left him lame, he retired and lived the rest of his life with Alice and her two children, first in Sharpness and later in Dursley. He was deeply religious, and I have in my possession his old seafaring Bible which is inscribed on the inside of the back cover (maybe as a christening present?) to my father in 1911, when he was not yet two years old.

By all accounts, Henry Atkins was a kind and wonderful man. My father used to speak of him often, and in my own pre-teenage years when he was teaching me DIY skills – carpentry, painting, mending all sorts of things – he would recount tales of his grandfather Henry who had taught him all these skills. He had a wealth of seafaring stories and was very interested in his grandchildren – perhaps because their own father was so often away. In my Edinburgh workshop, I still have Henry Atkins's huge old oak tool chest, complete with some of the marlin spikes, planes, hand-drills, chisels and other paraphernalia for everyday household repairs in the pre- and post-war era. Using them brings back memories of working with my father in our tool shed at Roselands. Happy days.

I think that my father's childhood was, for the most part, happy too. There was little money but a strong sense of community among the Sharpness seafarers. He also adored his grandfather. My father left school at the age of fourteen, as so many people did in those days, and went to work for RA Lister & Co. Twenty-five years later, when we moved to London, he had risen to be their works manager.

My father was a very keen sportsman – a 'small ball man' as he liked to say. He played hockey for Dursley, Stroud and Gloucestershire, along with tennis, cricket and golf. I believe that it was at the local tennis club that his close friend, Melbourne 'Bunny' Stear, introduced him to two sisters, Jane and Doreen Fletcher. Bunny married Jane and Bob married Doreen.

My mother, Doreen Stanger Fletcher, was born on 27 July 1914 at Attenborough, a village near Nottingham. The Fletchers are a large clan, and thanks to my great-uncle Fred, who helped his brother Samuel Billyeald compile a family history (*The Fletcher House of Lace*, Derwent Press, 1959) I can trace my own ancestry back through Edward and Phoebe Fletcher (who had eighteen children) to a Samuel Fletcher who was born in 1722. All of these ancestors lived in or near Nottingham – mostly just over the Derbyshire border at Heanor – and they became well-known in the nineteenth century for making high-quality lace. Artisans started investing in the then recently invented lace machines in the early 1800s, and the children of Edward and Phoebe Fletcher were pioneers in developing this new industry. It survived until the time of the First World War, when lace was largely replaced by synthetic materials.

I have lived more than half my life in Edinburgh, and from The Fletcher House of Lace I am delighted to learn that the Fletchers originated in Scotland. Prior to the lace trade, the Fletchers were arrow-makers (hence the name) and apparently made arrows for several of the Scottish clans – the Campbells and Stewarts in Argyllshire and the MacGregors in Perthshire. When Bonnie Prince Charlie's army abandoned plans to march on London and turned north again near Derby in 1745, some of the Fletchers settled locally and worked in the South Derbyshire coal mines before becoming involved in the altogether more decorous lace industry.

My maternal grandfather Robert Preston Fletcher (1886-1964) was the eldest of five children of Edward Henry Fletcher and Emma Jane (neé Preston). In my boyhood, I visited the latter, my great-grandmother, several times at Combe Martin, Devon, where she died, aged ninety-seven, in 1962. Grandfather Fletcher lived near Taunton in Somerset, where he had Airedale dogs, smoked a pungent pipe and played the violin rather badly. The son of a poultry farmer, he was a signaller in the First World War, after which he sold food products to farmers for a firm called Vitameal. Only in later years did I find out about the family scandal he had caused.

My mother grew up in Uley, a small village near Dursley. She was very much a country girl, enjoying the outdoors and all aspects of village life. She was the eldest of three – her sister Jane and brother Bobby, of whom she was particularly fond. I know very little about her parents' relationship. Her mother was rather formidable and in later life became something of a misandrist. Then again, she had good reason.

In 1933, life for the Fletcher family changed dramatically. My grandfather left the family home after falling in love with one of my mother's best friends, Hilda Kerrins (whom we always knew as 'K'). K was twenty-four, my mother eighteen and they had become close friends through running the local Girl Guide troop. Grandfather Fletcher was forty-seven. It's not for me to pass judgement on events, of which in any case I only know little, and these were very different times. All I can say is that I visited 'Grandma K', as we became used to calling her, in her little house in Wellington, Somerset in 1990. She was then eighty-two, and still the same shy, kind and self-effacing woman I had always known. She knew that I was going through a divorce at that time, and she wanted to share her story with me.

Grandma K was born in Wellington, India, in 1908 and – with remarkable symmetry – died in Wellington, Somerset in 2008. She had a rather sad and, I believe, lonely life, but was one of the most gentle and loving people I have ever met. She was a very private person and perhaps somewhat ashamed of her relationship with my grandfather, but – remarkably – remained a close friend of my mother throughout both their lives. She had a difficult childhood, contracting malaria at the age of three, and losing her father soon afterwards. Her mother then returned to England, leaving her behind in India before she was summoned to Herefordshire, where she was brought up by strangers. She worked as a governess and schoolteacher in Uley, where she met the Fletcher family.

She told me how she tried to reject my grandfather's advances, but even though she left Uley and entered nursing school at a hospital in East London, he pursued her, and eventually she gave in. My grandmother refused a divorce, so when they set up home in Somerset, grandfather at first passed her off as his niece. As the years went by, it was assumed that they were a couple and only after his death in 1964 was it revealed that she had never been married. This caused her considerable embarrassment.

I have one particularly happy memory of K towards the end of her life. When my cousin Michael Stear's daughter Samantha got married, I was assigned to collect K from her nursing home, take her to the wedding and look after her during the service and at the reception afterwards. I remember how light she was as I lifted her from my car to a seat on the lawn at the Stears' farm. When a waiter came round with drinks, I asked K if she would like some champagne or a soft drink. I assumed it would be the latter, but she enthusiastically took a glass of champagne and whispered to me, 'Make sure he comes round again soon!' She finished the first glass remarkably quickly and we both ended up with the giggles. Sometime before this, I had taken my daughters Sarah and Anna to meet K and, in a letter afterwards, she described her 'joy' at meeting them and said that they had 'much fun finding out each other's interests'. I was very touched that, though someone with very humble means, she left the girls five hundred pounds each in her will. A remarkable, generous and truly lovely person.

Villages being what they are, I can imagine that her father's behaviour must have cast a shadow over my mother's life, and that of all the family in Uley. Nevertheless, she took a job as a governess at The Gables, a splendid seventeenth-century Cotswold house on the edge of the village, and until marrying my father in 1936 was happy helping to look after orphans there. My parents married at St Mark's in Dursley on 28 July, 1936, one day after my mother's twenty-second birthday. My father was twenty-seven.

They decided to wait to have children until after the war, and despite the anxiety, the privations of rationing and other hardships, I believe that those war years were essentially happy for them both. While my father worked on at RA Lister, my mother took on various voluntary roles, including driving an ambulance. They took in evacuee children from London, and welcomed family and friends who were on leave, or recuperating from injury, to their small home. Then, as the war was coming to an end, my own life began.

2. SCHOOLDAYS

I first went to school at the age of five. Keble Preparatory School in Palmers Green was within walking distance of our home in Fox Lane, but my brother and I were small, so my mother would take us there on her bicycle, one sitting on the saddle, the other standing on the pedals and poor mother walking alongside pushing the handlebars. I do not remember much about my two years at Keble, but one highlight was my stage debut, playing the second moon in *The Song of Hiawatha* – a non-speaking part that required very little acting.

When we moved to Beaconsfield in 1952, I went to Davenies School from the age of seven to thirteen. I have many happy memories of those years. We were well taught in small classes and the teachers were disciplined but kind and interested in our development. I remember with particular gratitude Mrs Petty, who taught English and History. She loved Shakespeare, and every summer would put on a play in the small open-air theatre in a dell in the school grounds. My first role was as a fairy in *A Midsummer Night's Dream*. After small parts in *Julius Caesar* and *Henry IV*, I progressed to play Menenius in *Coriolanus* and, in my final summer, Bottom in a reprise of *A Midsummer Night's Dream*. I enjoyed

A 13-year-old Bottom in A Midsummer Night's Dream.

learning the lines for these productions and I believe this was an excellent grounding for the rote-learning that was necessary later in life when I studied biology and medicine. We were encouraged to take part in a lot of sports, and I played soccer, cricket and rugby for the school. I was also taught piano, violin, recorder and singing – but I will write about the importance of music to me in a separate chapter.

In choosing a secondary school, my parents followed the advice of the headmaster, Rev Newton, who was particularly keen on Bryanston School in Dorset. My parents had also been impressed by it and had already decided to send my brother there. A year later, in 1959, having passed the common entrance exam, I won a music scholarship and joined him. Over the years I have had many interviews, but my very first – for that scholarship – will always stay with me. I was interviewed by Thorold Coade, who had been Bryanston's headmaster for the previous twenty years, during which it had established its reputation as a leading public school. In my last year at prep school, I had been taught some rudimentary Greek. When Mr Coade asked me what subjects I particularly liked at school, I unwisely answered, 'The classics, sir.' To my horror, he then spoke to me in Greek. Having absolutely no idea what he meant, I answered with the only phrase I could remember – the title of the book from which we studied. Peering over his half-moon spectacles, he said, 'That's very good, Smyth. I shall look forward to seeing you in the autumn.'

It is difficult to summarise the experience of four years in a boarding school between the child-like age of thirteen and the pretence of being grown-up at eighteen, but for the most part these were very happy, exciting and rewarding years, and certainly some of the most important in my life.

Education at Bryanston was (and still is) founded on the Dalton Plan, an educational programme aimed at promoting pupils' independence, dependability and sense of responsibility to others. While classroom teaching remained important, we were expected – right from the outset – to organise and carry out assignments, working on our own, usually to a weekly timetable. In year one, classroom teaching took up three-quarters of the timetable, but by the sixth form we had only one or two classes a day, the rest being up to us to plan, research

Henley Royal Regatta, 1963. Bryanston losing to the King's School Canterbury, who went on to win the Princess Elizabeth Cup. I'm at No2.

My first season in the Bryanston 1st XV. I'm in the back row, third from the right.

and complete our allotted assignments. Our use of time and marks for completed work were recorded on a chart, which was reviewed once a week with the assigned tutor. For me, that was Rodney Dingle, a bachelor in his thirties who was a hero figure to us. He taught modern languages, had a remarkable knowledge of music which he used to train the school choir, and was head of rowing. His study, where I went for my weekly tutorial, had a wall lined with trophy oars he had won representing St John's, his Cambridge college, the university itself (in the 1952 Boat Race) and, with the same crew, Great Britain in international championships. He was an inspiring tutor – kind but demanding, but surprisingly tolerant when things were not up to his expectations, and very understanding about my family problem – of which more later.

After my voice broke and settled to a respectable lower bass, he encouraged me to consider trying for a choral scholarship to Cambridge, and arranged formal singing lessons. At my prep school I had enjoyed gym since we had an unusually good physical education teacher, and throughout my time at Bryanston I enjoyed PE under the guidance of Harold Tarraway, who had represented Great Britain in the 1948 Olympics and was a highly-regarded athletics coach. I played a lot of sports, especially rugby and rowing.

Rodney Dingle was in charge of rowing and delighted that I enjoyed it so much. The River Stour was a poor one for oarsmen, with too many bends and only a three-minute straight. I won cups for single sculling and racing in pairs as a junior, stroked the Colts VIII and rowed in the First VIII in 1963 in the Princess Elizabeth Cup at the

Henley Regatta. I still remember training for the summer rowing regattas, especially Henley. The First VIII were required to circuit-train twice a day – before breakfast and in the evening – and we rowed six afternoons a week throughout the summer term. To cope with this, we had a separate table in the dining room, where we were fed extra rations. Rowing at number two, I was the lightest member of the crew and our coaches were determined that no-one should weigh-in for Henley at under eleven stone. On the day itself, I hit the target exactly. After I left Bryanston, I kept in touch with Rodney and over the years we became friends. He died in 2017 at the age of eighty-seven and is missed by me and many others whose young lives he nourished.

The other teacher at Bryanston for whom I have particular gratitude was my housemaster, Richard Hunter, known to all as Bunty. He was another inspirational character, perhaps all the more surprising for the fact that he had led a rather restricted life. A lifelong bachelor, he was himself a former pupil and head boy at Bryanston, and returned to teach there shortly after university. He was only fifty when he died from lung cancer – although he had never been a non-smoker and was always fit. By the time of his illness, I was a consultant at the Royal Marsden Hospital specialising in lung cancer, but almost all our treatments were experimental. I last saw him when I visited St Bartholomew's Hospital in London on 27 November 1977, the day that my daughter Sarah was born. He died the following week. At school he gave me my first lessons in Spanish, and particularly encouraged me to play rugby. I had two seasons in the First XV and played in the schools seven-a-side team at the Roehampton tournament in 1963. In my last year I was captain of our house and therefore spent a lot of time in Bunty's company. He had a strict but very paternalistic approach to housemastering and taught me a lot about the requirements and methods of good leadership, which have served me well in my subsequent career in academic medicine. We always kept in touch, and I am humbled by a letter that he wrote to me in 1972 thanking me for 'being so cheerful and friendly and also for teaching me so much about my job!'

Largely due to all the rowing and rugby I did at school, I developed a lifelong enthusiasm for keeping fit. For more than four decades, I have been a member of the Edinburgh Club, a gym run by Scottish judo expert George Kerr CBE, one of only seven people in the world to be awarded the tenth Dan, the highest level in judo. I have never taken up judo, but for the past twenty years George has been my personal trainer, and despite this we remain very good friends. He enjoys teasing me, but I console myself with thinking how be much less flexible and fit, I would be if not for our twice-weekly sessions, which I greatly missed during the Covid pandemic.

For most of my time at Bryanston I was really happy. I was well taught, enjoyed studying and all the sport and music enriched my life. I also made lifelong friends and should mention two in particular. Robin Pegna has been a very close friend ever since we met at the age of fourteen. We have been as close as brothers and have helped each other through all sorts of highs and lows at Cambridge, where Robin read economics and sang in the King's College choir, and through the many years of work and family life ever since. He is godfather to my eldest daughter, Sarah, and was my best man at my marriage to Ann. Even longer suffering amongst my friends from schooldays is Robin Goodman, with whom I rowed in the pairs, shared a study, and later, rooms at Trinity College for our first and third years. We are still in touch and sat together at the Trinity annual gathering just a few months ago. I have remained in touch with Bryanston over the years and in 1979 was proposed by Launcelot Fleming to join its board of governors. I served in this capacity for thirty-five years, only resigning in 2014 (though I had offered to stand down many times). Despite the distance from Edinburgh, I was able to offer advice on some important occasions and my fellow governors were generous in their tolerance of me.

There were also, however, difficult times during my schooldays resulting from my father's mental health and subsequent alcoholism. It does not seem appropriate to dwell on this now, but a brief summary is contextual to several aspects of my adult life.

Around 1956-7 my father began to suffer from depression and anxiety. Although to the outside world his work at Buckingham Gate was very successful, he was challenged by the dramatic expansion of the business driven by John and his brother Gerald Panchaud, who had moved to live in Switzerland. Their company had become more and more international and my father travelled to Brussels, Paris, Berlin and Rotterdam, but felt insecure in not speaking foreign languages. He also felt – inappropriately – inferior to the company's new directors who had all had a university education. In the summer of 1957, aged only forty-eight, he resigned on the grounds of ill health and never formally worked again. What was then called a nervous breakdown was diagnosed as depression, but I believe that he suffered more from severe anxiety. He was treated with electroconvulsive therapy – which he hated, and from which he seemed to achieve little benefit. He resorted to alcohol.

I was in my last two years at preparatory school, and from then until I was in my last year at Cambridge, his alcoholism became a major problem for my mother, my brother and me. I could not bring schoolfriends home because he would be drunk and abusive – verbally, never physically. I was embarrassed when he would turn up at school sports events unsteady on his feet and with slurred speech. I was ashamed of him and there were times when I actually hated him. I knew that he was proud of me for my sporting achievements and for getting into university, but having so much enjoyed his company in my pre-teen years when he taught me his manual skills, I could not understand him letting himself down so much by his alcoholism. I was glad to get away to a boarding school, and when in due course my tutor, housemaster and closest friends at Bryanston learnt about my father's behaviour they all showed kindness and understanding.

Things came to a head at Christmas in 1966. Longstanding friends of my parents, Walter Coleman and his wife Sheila, were staying with us. Walter had been in the Army during the war and had seen plenty of drunkenness. After a particularly awful evening, he told my father that his behaviour was completely unacceptable and insisted that he seek professional help. With Walter's assistance, father was referred to a David Stafford-Clark, a well-known psychiatrist at Guy's Hospital in

London. For the next three months he was an in-patient at Guy's York Clinic.

He emerged a changed man. I remember going home at Easter, having not seen him since Christmas. He was quiet, withdrawn and remote. There were occasional lapses in subsequent years, but he never returned to his previous heavy drinking and gradually recovered his normal state – and we became friends again.

Throughout my schooldays, music became increasingly important to me. Much of this was down to my brother Robert. As children, we were very close, sharing a bedroom at home until our late teenage years. We also had many adventures together. When I was fourteen, for example, we cycled on an old tandem from our house in Beaconsfield to our great-uncle Eric's house in Combe Martin, Devon. It took us five or six days, camping overnight with equipment that had to be carried on the back of the bike. We also had a canoe and spent many idyllic days together on the Thames, but it was a shared love of music that really bound us together.

I do not know from where our musicality came from as neither of our parents were musical, but from the age of five when Robert sat in front of a piano, it was immediately obvious that he had a natural talent. In fact, it was more than that: he was a musical prodigy. By the time he was thirteen, when he won a music scholarship to Bryanston, he could play most of the Beethoven piano sonatas and a full repertoire of Liszt and Chopin pieces. Throughout his time at school, he was a regular performer at school concerts; in his final term, he played the Schumann Piano Concerto with the school orchestra to great acclaim.

*First time in morning dress. With my parents and Robert
for our cousin Heather's wedding.*

When he subsequently went to the Royal Academy of
Music in London he was, of course, amongst other equally
talented young people. He won the performer's prize at
the end of his first year there but from then on never
progressed. All my life I have striven to work hard and
achieve, but Robert did not have the same motivation.
Perhaps music came too easily for him in the beginning:
certainly, he never put in the hard graft to perfect pieces
which is essential for any professional musician. He had a
natural flair for light music, and after a spell teaching in a
girls' school, resorted to earning a sort of living playing

in clubs, pubs and cruise liners. I was greatly saddened at such a wasted opportunity, but Robert's drive to achieve more simply was not there.

The reason for describing his early remarkable talent is that, fond of him as I was, it had a negative effect on my own musical development. Music has been, and always will be, of inestimable importance to me but, faced with such a talented brother, any improvements I made as a result of my piano lessons seemed pathetic by comparison. I gave up at the age of eight and a couple of years later took up the violin, while he carried on towards a potential career as a musician. After two years at Bryanston, I sat my O-levels – a mixture of sciences, languages, English and maths. At A-level, I opted for biology, chemistry and physics. In my last term, I prepared for the Cambridge entrance exams and sat papers in zoology and botany, for which I was offered a place at Trinity Hall. Looking back, it now seems very restrictive to have to choose such a limited range of subjects at the age of sixteen– essentially, it's either science or the humanities. I was delighted, many years later, to find that my daughters, educated in Scotland, had a far wider choice under the Scottish system of Highers. In the 1960s, only a small proportion of school leavers went on to university, so naturally we were all encouraged to think about future careers at an early stage. My favourite subjects were biology and chemistry, and while many of my classmates opted for medicine, I decided – with remarkably little real knowledge of the subject – on a career in biochemistry. One of the things that put me off medicine was the length of training it would require, and that thought was influenced by another major event for my sixteen-year-old self.

I fell in love.

On a rare family holiday in Spain in the summer of 1962 I met Anna, a distant second cousin. We were both sixteen, but while I was preparing for my A-levels, she had just left school and was working for a modelling agency. She had a beautiful face, a 36-23-36 figure, and introduced me to sex. I was besotted, and we fell passionately in love. On the few occasions she was able to visit me at school or come to a regatta, my friends (and, I think, some of the staff) could not believe my luck. They say that the first time that you fall in love stays with you forever, but after the extraordinary highs of the time we spent together during school holidays at her parents' home near Coventry, a devastating blow was awaiting me.

In December 1963 I won a choral exhibition to Trinity College, Cambridge and left school, allowing a nine-month gap before going to university. I hoped to spend all of that time with Anna, but she decided that our relationship had to end. I was heartbroken. She wanted to be married and said that waiting three or four years until I left Cambridge was too long. (There was no question of undergraduates getting married in those days). To be dismissed in this way was probably the lowest point in my life to date. I was desolated.

During my last year at school my parents moved from Beaconsfield to Romsey in Hampshire, partly to give my father a new start, but also to be near my mother's sister Jane, who lived in nearby Winchester. From 1963 to 1967 we lived at Belbins House, just outside Romsey. The house itself was not particularly special, but it sat in seven acres of grounds. The property was originally a showpiece for a landscape gardening company, with the house having been extended from the gardener's cottage. Four acres were woodland and the rest well-planned gardens. It was a wonderful place, though isolated, and I was upset at losing Anna. I could not stay there just waiting to go to Cambridge in the autumn – but what was I to do?

I was rescued by my godfather, John Panchaud. He was living in Switzerland, but on a business trip to London invited me to have lunch with him at a very posh hotel in Sloane Street. When I told him that I intended to study biochemistry at Cambridge, he asked if I would like to get some practical experience in the months between school and university. The youngest of his four children had been born with cystic fibrosis, a horrid disease – often fatal, and for which there was little treatment in those days. With the help of wealthy friends, Uncle John (as I called him) founded the Cystic Fibrosis Research Foundation Trust, based at the famous Great Ormond Street Hospital for sick children. It continues to this day.

He arranged for me to meet the head of chemical pathology, Dr (later Professor Dame) Barbara Clayton, who offered me the chance to spend several months as an assistant to one of her PhD students. This was a most enjoyable and useful time. I learnt practical skills of chromatography and spectroscopy, which came in handy not only at Cambridge also but years later when I was doing research for my MD thesis at the Institute of Cancer Research. Robert had a job at Harrods, and we shared a garret flat in Ebury Street, Belgravia. Uncle John then invited us to visit him in his château at

Morges on Lake Geneva.

After my stint at Great Ormond Street, the two of us borrowed our mother's car – a Morris Minor Traveller – and set off on one of our best adventures together. We drove through France, Germany, and Austria – where we had a wonderful time in Salzburg – then down into Italy, first to Venice and later to the coast, where we camped on the seashore near Ancona. We continued over the Apennines south-west to Rome before heading north to Switzerland and Lake Geneva. The contrast of having been camping for several weeks followed by the luxury of Uncle John's château was dramatic and a bit daunting, but his staff kindly washed our clothes and our car and made us feel a little more presentable. A highlight of this visit was one evening when my godfather drove us at great speed in his Ferrari round the north side of Lake Geneva to a nightclub in Lausanne. We both felt incredibly grown-up!

This whole trip was a great finish to the interlude between school and university. Reflecting now on my godfather, I recognise that John Panchaud was something of a hero figure to me, the first true entrepreneur I ever knew. One of his ventures was in Scotland, when together with his brother Gerald, in 1962 they bought a Deeside Victorian lodge and estate next to the Queen's Scottish residence, Balmoral. Apparently on a business trip to New York, my godfather had shared an evening tasting Scottish malt whiskies. In those days blended whisky was often drunk with soda water, but malts were served with small amounts of still water. The Americans complained that New York tap water tasted of chlorine, and the only available bottled water was the French Perrier, which was aerated. On returning to the UK, Uncle John shared with my father his brilliant idea to bottle Scottish spring water and market it in the US to improve the experience of drinking malt whisky. My father thought he was mad, but what vision! Nowadays every supermarket has shelves full of bottled water from many sources, but this was the early 1960s. My godfather and his brother bought Mar Lodge and its estate at Braemar, turned it into a luxury hotel and built a bottling plant. Both expert skiers as a result of their years in Switzerland, they bought huge snowmaking machines to develop a ski resort. This never really succeeded. Nineteen-sixty-two had been one of the coldest winters on record, with huge amounts of snow, but the next few years were milder, the slopes were south-facing and not very high, and this part of the venture failed. However, the hotel was a huge success, and so was the water. Early on in this enterprise, the Panchauds asked my father if he would consider moving us all to Braemar so that he could be in residence to oversee the whole project. My father took the long train journey to Aberdeen, and investigated the project's possibilities, but he declined their offer, mostly on the grounds of Mar Lodge's remoteness. I remember him discussing this with me, then aged sixteen, and his account of the place's most spectacular feature – a ballroom with 2,400 stags' heads on the wall. Last year Ann and I went to find Mar Lodge, now a National Trust property and the stags' heads are still there. Sadly, John Panchaud died from colon cancer in 1974 when he was only fifty-eight, but his brother kept the estate until his own death in 1989.

The Panchaud brothers were a truly remarkable pair, and I was very fortunate to have such an inspiring godfather.

3. CAMBRIDGE 1964-67

In early October 1964 I went up to Cambridge and started three wonderful years at Trinity College. I had rooms in New Court, which I shared with Robin Goodman, a friend from Bryanston. I realised immediately one of the great advantages of being a choral exhibitioner, since I immediately made friends with students in the years ahead of me, and through the choir practices, services and chapel life in general, quickly felt part of that extraordinary college.

I threw myself into everything I could – playing in the college orchestra, playing rugby for the Second XV, rowing, and applying to join the university's air squadron. My cousin Michael Stear, who had been at Emmanuel College, recommended that I do the latter, not just because I would learn to fly but because its headquarters in Chaucer Road was the best club in town and sold beer at rock-bottom prices. The recruitment process was very thorough – aptitude tests, medicals and interviews – but by the end of that first term I was accepted. I was thrilled. In the summer term I rowed for Trinity and really enjoyed the bump races. In years two and three, flying two or three times a week made rugby and rowing impossible, but I had enjoyed tasting both as

The Chapel of Trinity College Cambridge.

My cousin Michael Stear in his flying days.

part of college life. I owe a lot more to cousin Michael than just introducing me to flying. Throughout my life he has been like an older brother. While at school he encouraged me to play rugby and to row (both of which he was very good at) and he taught me how to fish. He himself used the University Air Squadron as a launch pad for a stellar career in the RAF. He was an exceptional pilot and rose through the ranks to the very top, becoming Air Chief Marshal Sir Michael Stear KCB CBE DL, Deputy Commander-in-Chief, Allied Forces Central Europe. He died two years ago and I miss him greatly.

The one thing that did not go well in my first year was studying. For my planned degree in biochemistry, I needed to pass a major exam in three science subjects at the end of my second year in the three-year course. On the advice of my director of studies, I enrolled in physiology, invertebrate zoology, and organic chemistry. The first two were fine, but the lectures in chemistry were poor and my supervisor in college was a PhD student who wasn't a good teacher. I was disappointed to get a third in the end of year exams and started to seriously question whether I was starting my career in the right direction.

The summer vacation at Cambridge lasts for three months and I had decided to go to North America. Through the British Universities North American Club, I was able to buy a return flight to New York and an open travel ticket for the Greyhound bus network for just £50. I would, however, need to work to pay for living expenses. Astonishingly, the only way to obtain a work visa in those days was to formally emigrate. This involved filling in countless forms, showing birth certificates, and attending the US embassy in London for blood tests, a chest X-ray and a rather confrontational interview. This was conducted by a fierce woman who questioned my reasons for wanting to emigrate to the US, particularly as I had every intention of returning to the UK in the autumn to continue my studies at Cambridge. However, the main thing they were concerned with was whether I had proof of a job to go to. My friendship with Bishop Launcelot Fleming helped enormously in this regard. I will write about him later, but one of Launcelot's many friends was Gerry Frank, the co-owner of a large department store, Meier & Frank, in Portland, Oregon. With Launcelot's introduction, I was offered work in the store and had a letter to meet all the immigration requirements.

I flew from Gatwick in mid-July and returned at the end of September after the biggest adventure of my life so far. I'm glad that I still have a diary in which I recorded those extraordinary ten weeks. On 19 July, I boarded a Greyhound bus in Manhattan to take me all the way to Los Angeles. I spent three days and three nights on that bus – which stopped every two to three hours for a change of driver and restroom for the passengers but otherwise pushed on remorselessly across the continent. I did not have the time to visit any of the cities and towns en route, but I did want to see Los Angeles and the West Coast before taking up the short-term job awaiting me in Portland. My main recollection of this journey was of the extraordinary size of North America. I have flown from coast to coast many times since, but nothing can impress upon you the scale of the distances involved more than travelling by road. From New York we journeyed through Pennsylvania to Pittsburgh, with its huge steel industry, to Columbia, Ohio, and on to Indianapolis. Across the Mississippi, we travelled through Missouri to Tulsa in Oklahoma. All my life I have enjoyed westerns, and it was amazing to see at first hand the vastness of New Mexico and Arizona and to recognise the landscape from the films. We arrived in Los Angeles at 3am, and I was glad to find a nearby hotel and a bed to sleep in. A few days later I was in Portland and began working at Meier & Frank, where I was assigned to the men's outfitting department. For the next two months I had a really enjoyable time. The work was easy and I made several friends. Of the latter I particularly remember John McFadden, whose parents had a cabin and speedboat on the Columbia River to the north of the city. We spent several weekends there. John was an excellent water-skier and taught me the rudiments of the sport, which was great fun. Most of the young men working in the store that summer were subsequently called up for the Vietnam War, and tragically John was killed there the following year.

One evening quite early in my time in Portland I had what could be called an epiphany. I had been invited to a barbecue party by a lake somewhere just outside the town, and I fell into conversation with an elderly retired professor of modern languages from Vienna. He was interested in my dilemma: when I went back to Cambridge, should it be to study music, biochemistry, or – as I was increasingly thinking – medicine? I don't know who this man was, and I never met him again, but the hour I spent talking to him changed my life.

I told him I was meant to be studying biochemistry

but I didn't think I was good enough at science. I was toying with anthropology, but that was probably only because I'd just read a small book on the subject: it was probably just a passing whim. Music would appeal, but surely it would be too much of a risk? I shrugged, embarrassed by indecisiveness.

'Why not medicine?' he asked me, in heavily accented German that years of living in America had somehow left untouched. 'You've clearly got an interest in people and science. It would make perfect sense. Certainly, if I had my time again, that's what I'd do myself.' He was so certain, so direct: I couldn't help but pay attention. After all, I'd never had this kind of conversation with my parents, relatives, the Panchauds, or anyone at Cambridge. Yet here, on the other side of the world, sitting in a deckchair on a warm August night and talking to a complete stranger, a different future started to come into focus.

He'd had a good career, he said, but he'd always really wanted to study medicine. He would have done too, but the Second World War and emigration got in the way. A valid excuse, I thought. What was mine? As I walked back to the hotel, I realised that I didn't have any. I would, I decided that night, be a doctor.

Back then, Americans were much less used to English accents than they are today – so much so that customers would come up to my counter at Meier & Frank and ask how I was or even just to say something in my strange, but clearly alluring limey accent. Because of this – and absolutely not because of any knowledge of clothing trends among young Americans – I was called upon to be the compere for the store's 'back to college' fashion show in a local theatre. With guidance, I wrote a script but when I arrived at the venue, I found that the lighting was so poor that I could not read a word. I had to ad lib and was almost certainly awful, but – God bless America – everyone was very kind at the party afterwards.

I left Portland in mid-September and, back on the Greyhound bus, travelled east to Salt Lake City, where I visited the Mormon Temple, then on to Wyoming – real cowboy country. From there, we went through Nebraska and up the Platte River to Omaha, eventually reaching Chicago. It was then only a short journey to Detroit, where I stayed for a few days with Tom Akeley, the chaplain of Caius College in Cambridge. He was a good cello player and we had met earlier in the year playing in a small chamber orchestra conducted by John Eliot Gardiner.

On the way back to New York, I stopped at Niagara Falls, which was awesome but over-commercialised. In New York itself, I visited the United Nations building, where my elder stepdaughter Gillian now works – I love such interwoven connections across the decades. And so back to the UK. A remarkable and very memorable summer.

My second year at Cambridge was hectic but more enjoyable than my first. After visiting Launcelot Fleming – both to report on my American trip and, more importantly, to sound him out about my decision to read medicine, I was relieved to also gain the approval and encouragement of my tutor, Harry Williams, the dean of chapel, and my new director of studies, Dr Pat Merton. On the latter's advice, I opted for a busy second year of study, with less pressure in my final one.

Punting up to Grantchester for breakfast after the 1967 May Ball.

To be eligible for medical school after Cambridge, I had to add pathology and biochemistry to the physiology, zoology and chemistry I had taken in my first year. This meant being examined in five subjects rather than the customary three at the end of my second year. Then in my third year, all that I would have to do was anatomy. I was motivated and ready to work hard.

In the 1960s, Addenbrooke's Hospital in Cambridge did not offer clinical training for medical students, so after the three-year Natural Sciences Tripos with the prescribed pre-clinical subjects, students had to enrol in one of the London teaching hospitals for three years of clinical study, before returning to Cambridge for final exams. I applied to several of the London hospitals and was offered places at Saint George's and St Bartholomew's. I knew very little of either, but partly on the recommendation of my cousin Michael Stear (who had just got engaged to a lovely Barts nurse) I opted for Saint Bartholomew's. It turned out to be an excellent choice.

My middle year at Cambridge was full of music and flying, of which I will write separately, but apart from securing a place in medical school, one of the most life-changing events occurred in the spring of 1966. I fell in love again. And this time it was the real McCoy.

I met Dorothy Wood through mutual friends in the college choir. She was doing a teacher training year at Hughes Hall before becoming a biology teacher. She had an excellent soprano voice, for which she was much in demand, both in Cambridge and afterwards when we went to London. We became inseparable for the second half of my time in Cambridge, and she was a wonderful support to me throughout my clinical training and early years as a doctor in London. All told, we were together for six years. Everyone expected us to get married and it was only my uncertainties about my future direction in medicine and an inexplicable fear of commitment that prevented this. She subsequently married a delightful banker/musician, and has had a happy and successful family life. We are still in touch and remain good friends.

For my final undergraduate year in Cambridge, I had rooms in Trinity Great Court, again shared with Robin Goodman. I enjoyed being secretary of the college's Musical Society, was senior cadet in the air squadron (my first after-dinner speech was at its annual dinner: I can still remember how nervous I felt) and sang the lead role in a short Schubert opera for the May Week concert. Workwise, I spent all three terms dissecting a human body, which was, frankly, not the most efficient learning process and one now abandoned in most medical schools. However, the exam at the end of it went well and I finished with a 2:1 degree.

As the Count in Schubert's opera The Conspirators
with Dorothy Wood, May Week, Cambridge 1967

4. LAUNCELOT FLEMING

One of the most remarkable friendships I have ever had was with Bishop Launcelot Fleming (1906-90) – later appointed Dean of Windsor by the Queen – and I will always be grateful for his wisdom, kindness and advice. I was one of his many friends – indeed in *Friends for Life*, an aptly titled 1981 biography of him to which I was privileged to contribute, he is recorded as having received over 3,000 Christmas cards in one year alone!

I first met Launcelot while at Bryanston, where he was a governor, and we remained in close touch for twenty-seven years until his death in 1990. The son of Robert Fleming, a distinguished doctor in Edinburgh, Launcelot became a famous geologist and clergyman. At Trinity Hall in Cambridge, he discovered a lifelong interest in geology (for which he got a first-class degree), enthusiasm for rowing (for which he subsequently became an inspiring coach), and confusion about whether or not to be ordained. On graduating, he studied at Westcott House, the Anglican theological college in Cambridge, and then became chaplain back at Trinity Hall. However, during his training as an ordinand, he was invited to be the geologist on two expeditions to the Arctic, so during his first year as Trinity Hall's chaplain, he joined the British

Graham Land Expedition of 1934-37 to Antarctica.

He spent two winters in the Antarctic in the company of only fifteen other men, whom he also served as chaplain. This experience deepened his Christian faith: as he wrote, 'A man sees himself here as he really is and not as he wants other people to believe him to be.' This three-year expedition was later recognised as having been of major importance in the history of Antarctic exploration, and in 1940 King George VI conferred the Polar Medal on all its members. As a clergyman, Fleming's career was stellar: after sixteen years as fellow, chaplain and dean of his beloved Trinity Hall, he was appointed Bishop of Portsmouth at the age of only forty-three. He subsequently became Bishop of Norwich and in 1971 was invited by the Queen to be her domestic chaplain as Dean of Windsor.

Launcelot Fleming with the Royal Family, Windsor 1975

I was introduced to Launcelot through his friendship with my tutor at Bryanston, Rodney Dingle. Like Rodney, Launcelot was passionate about rowing and during the Easter holidays in 1963 he invited the First VIII to spend a few days at his home in Norwich. Ostensibly this was to help with team-building before the summer regattas, but there was a second agenda. The bishop's house in Norwich had a large garden, most of which was wild and uncultivated, and the eight of us were required to spend the mornings hacking away at the undergrowth with scythe and pitchfork. In the afternoons we would go to the beach to swim in the icy North Sea and play games on the beach. The evenings were for 'companionship' – one of Launcelot's favourite words. He was a great believer in physical fitness and a competitive sportsman. A strong swimmer, his tennis court was permanently in use, and he was a formidable squash player. He especially enjoyed playing me at squash as I was really bad at it – he always won.

What first impressed me about him was his wonderful capacity to communicate with people of all ages – especially the young – and his passionate belief in the connection between an active spiritual and physical life. He also had an extraordinary ability to organise his time. I had never met anyone who had such a busy life but who could nevertheless down tools for sometimes a ridiculously short period – maybe only half an hour – during a busy week, and be completely relaxed during that time, diverting his mental and physical energies to some form of active recreation which would visibly recharge his batteries.

After that first visit to Norwich, I called on him many

times when I was an undergraduate at Cambridge, and again was struck by how calmly and clearly he organised his time. He would write to say that he would be delighted to see me between two-thirty and four o'clock on a particular afternoon a month ahead. When I arrived, I would realise just how precise that timescale had to be, but also how completely he would appear to relax and set aside the mental pressures of the rest of his working day. He seemed to genuinely enjoy the company of other people as an active way of coping with his own, very hectic life, although he also contributed hugely to the lives of those around him. It was a remarkable honour for a young undergraduate to be taken into his confidence on matters about which I was usually ignorant, yet he made you feel that, for a moment at least, you were the most important person to him. It was certainly quite out of proportion to any contribution that I was able to reciprocate.

I remember several visits to Norwich in the mid-1960s when he was particularly active in the House of Lords discussions on youth policy. He would frequently ask for my advice about speeches he was proposing to make or for comments on his contribution in Hansard. I remember several occasions when, following an evening of discussion in his study, just as I was going to bed, he would produce some lengthy speech, or notes for a speech, and ask me to glance through it before I went to sleep so that we could discuss it over breakfast. His concept of 'glancing through' would usually involve a fairly thorough interrogation over the bacon and eggs. I don't believe that I ever contributed significantly to the content of the work in which he was involved, but the exercise seemed to help him to rehearse his thoughts and was intellectually stimulating for me.

As a result of these discussions, I came to feel a deep sense of affection for Launcelot and indeed to see him in something of a surrogate father role. There were two occasions in my life when I particularly sought his advice about major decisions, and it was through some of these early meetings in Norwich that I learnt to respect his wisdom and judgement. The first was at the beginning of my second year in Cambridge, when I was looking for reassurance that the idea of becoming a doctor made sense. Knowing how busy Launcelot was, I remember sheepishly phoning his secretary to ask if there was any chance of seeing him. She made the usual polite holding manoeuvres, but I soon got an instruction from Launcelot to visit him in Norwich. His ability to relate to someone so many years younger than himself, and to fully understand my dilemma helped me to resolve the issue in my own mind in a way that led me to believe that I had made the choice myself and had in no way had a decision imposed upon me.

The second occasion came thirteen years later when faced with a major career decision that I could not resolve. I had been offered two hugely important jobs at the same time – the chair of medical oncology in Edinburgh and the chair of medicine at the Royal Marsden Hospital. I remembered our remarkable conversation all those years ago in Norwich and how helpful Launcelot had been and decided to phone him at his home in Sherborne. I had not in fact contacted him for several months and I remember asking his wife Jane whether I might speak to Launcelot for a lengthy chat. He came to the phone, and I briefly outlined that I needed to discuss something of considerable importance to me. He then paused to get pencil and paper and we spent nearly an hour and a half on the phone when once again his remarkable ability to put someone else first and to counsel me as a true friend was humbling. There are many people who enjoy giving advice, and it is always flattering to be asked to do so, but Launcelot had his extraordinary way of leading a conversation without being directive, allowing people to see the rights and wrongs of situations for themselves.

Over my years as a professor of medicine I have tutored and mentored many students and trainees. Never achieving the remarkable skills that Launcelot had, I nevertheless learnt so much from him, and have tried to develop and use those lessons myself. I have kept many of the letters he wrote to me and realise how fortunate I was to have his friendship and guidance over so many years.

In the summer of 1967 Launcelot was faced with the biggest challenge of his life. Quite suddenly while playing tennis one afternoon, he lost the use of his left leg. Soon he could use neither leg and was admitted to the National Hospital for Nervous Diseases in Queen Square, London. Over the course of several months, it proved difficult to secure a diagnosis: I believe now that he must have suffered from some form of transverse myelitis. With extensive physiotherapy, his condition slowly improved. He left hospital needing two sticks with which to hobble but eventually got by with one. Barely able to walk, his greatest sadness was the realisation that his competitive sporting days were over. He could, however, still swim.

I remember subsequent outings with him to the

swimming pool at Dolphin Square, where his remarkable determination to overcome physical disability could be seen in his face as he would swim to the point of exhaustion in spite of being unable to use his legs. I was humbled by his ability to accept sympathy in a positive and sincere way, thus avoiding any embarrassment and even making me feel that I was contributing and helping him, which in reality I was so little able to do. In 1971, the Queen appointed Launcelot to be the Dean of Windsor. The role included being her domestic chaplain and therefore a member of the Royal Household. I visited Launcelot several times when he was in Windsor and most of those visits are coloured in my memory by his physical disability. I remember one afternoon in the autumn of 1972 when I visited him in Windsor Castle, and we went swimming in the Queen's swimming pool. He delighted in showing me some quite extraordinary equipment which the Royal Family used for practising polo indoors – a sort of artificial horse. Launcelot became almost completely exhausted after his swim and was clearly finding his physical disability extremely difficult. It was a long, arduous walk back to his study in the deanery, where we sat for a long time having a conversation about his present predicament and reflecting on the effects of immobility on his life. It was one of the few times that I can remember when he spoke at length about his own problems.

Although he was extremely discreet about his relationship with the Royal Family, it was clear that he got to know many of them very well – and the respect was mutual. When he retired in 1976, the Queen created him a Knight Commander of the Royal Victorian Order.

Launcelot died in 1990, more than three decades ago, yet I still think of him often, and continually try to apply some of the many lessons of life he taught me. The quote from Hardy's *The Woodlanders* with which Donald Lindsay concludes his *Friends for Life* biography is, I think, particularly apt: 'No, I never can forget 'ee. For you was a good man and did good things.'

5. LEARNING TO FLY

Music apart, of all the recreational activities I have been fortunate to enjoy – all sports, all travel, and all hobbies – none has given me greater pleasure than learning to fly. Taking to the sky in a small plane, either alone or with one or two friends, is a wonderful, life-enhancing experience. I've been doing it for fifty-five years and I hope to continue for as long as my health allows.

Every flight brings a small sense of achievement. Light aircraft flying is very safe, if done properly: if you have prepared adequately, your plane is well maintained, and you know where you are going, the fact that you are taking your life in your hands rewards you with experiences that nothing else can. You are totally dependent on yourself. Much has been written about the freedom of the skies, but in a small, single-engine aircraft – especially an open-cockpit biplane – it has to be experienced to be believed.

Apart from the obvious joy of being up there among (but always clear of) the clouds, there are aspects of learning to fly that have resonated closely with other parts of my life – both private and professional.

Flying teaches you above all else the importance of thorough preparation. Flight planning, checking the maintenance record of your aircraft, thoroughly checking the plane on the ground, checking the weather and so on, are all lessons that have relevance to carefully preparing teaching lessons, or scientific presentations for international conferences. Learning how to navigate is naturally relevant to planning journeys by other means – and I still avoid using the 'toys' provided in modern cars lest they should malfunction and leave you lost, and there's nothing wrong with an old-fashioned map! The need for safety in an aircraft is obvious, but it has given me a lifelong awareness of the needs for vigilance in other settings such as being in a small boat or hiking in unfamiliar territory. One of the lesser realised benefits of putting your own (and others') life at risk in a potentially dangerous environment, is the concentration required. When I am flying, I have to concentrate a hundred per cent on the task at hand. While enjoying the beauty of nature in all its aspects, there is an absolute requirement to focus on your plane and how you are flying it. There is no room for letting your mind wander onto other things – as one constantly does on terra firma. The result is that far from finding a flight tiring, I very often feel refreshed afterwards – as though I have given my brain a reboot, only tasking it with one thing at a time. Modern life is so constantly interrupted by mobile phones, emails, social media of all sorts, that to be able to commit to a single task for an hour or so is a blessing. I recommend flying as the antidote to all this.

As I have already mentioned, being taught to fly as a member of the Cambridge University Air Squadron was a major commitment during my three years as an undergraduate. We were expected to go out to Marshall's

Airfield two or three times a week for flying training and to attend the HQ in Chaucer Road one evening a week during term time for ground school instruction. All this RAF training led up to taking the Preliminary Flying Badge (PFB) – a sort of junior wings award, which is much more demanding than a civilian private pilot's licence. We were examined in all the ground school activities, such as meteorology, navigation, and air law. Then there was the practical stuff: instrument rating, solo night flying, and hard flying tests which involved all the routine aspects of flying plus aerobatics and spinning. The Chipmunks on which we learnt, tail-wheeled aircraft with a tandem cockpit – pilot in front and instructor behind – were great to fly, and quite a lot of emphasis was placed on teaching us basic aerobatic skills such as loops, barrel and slow rolls, stall turns, and figures of eight. The purpose of this was not to make us display pilots or – heaven forbid – to show off, but to make us fully confident in any situation that we might find ourselves in. 'The plane is strapped to you,' my instructor used to say. 'You are not just sitting in it!'

Every pilot remembers their first solo. Mine was in May 1965 after just over fourteen hours of dual instruction. Every year we were required to spend between two and four weeks on a 'summer camp' at a working RAF station to introduce us to real life in the RAF. These were great fun, and we were paid as well! My first camp was at Bicester, my second at Wattisham and my third at Tangmere, where I passed the flying test for my PFB. Through a fortunate administrative error, I was allowed a full year with the London University Air Squadron when I started my clinical training at Barts, so all in all over

Acting Pilot Officer Smyth, RAFVR 1967

four years I clocked up just under two hundred hours' flying time. It was only when I subsequently took a private pilot's licence and joined civilian flying clubs that I fully appreciated what superb training I had had, and I have been very grateful ever since.

The first flying club that I joined while I was a student at Barts was the Tiger Club, based at Redhill. The Tiger Moth is much more difficult to fly well than the Chipmunk. With fewer instruments, no brakes or flaps and with only a tail skid, it is surprisingly difficult to see forward while taxiing or on final approach just before landing. But what an exciting experience it is to be up there in an open-cockpit – especially doing aerobatics! The Tiger Moth loops very easily but it is difficult to roll, given its four large wings and small ailerons. Upside down, the Tiger's engine cuts out – as does the Chipmunk's – since there is no inverted fuel system. Hanging in your straps, still trying to keep your feet on the rudder pedals requires good abdominal muscles. The engine restarts when you point the aircraft towards the ground and gather speed, so rolls were rather quick, not slow! I was very fortunate indeed to be allowed to fly a famous Tiger Moth biplane G-ACDC, the oldest plane on the British register, built in 1933. My logbook shows thirty-two hours flying it, twenty-eight of them solo.

All pilots make (occasional) mistakes – and you learn from them. One such lesson was when I nearly ran out of fuel in this very precious aircraft. In October 1977 I had been invited to participate in a small international conference at the magnificent medieval Leeds Castle, near Maidstone in Kent. I estimated that it was about thirty minutes' flying time from Redhill, and it would be fun to overfly the castle to take some souvenir photographs. I booked the first sortie of the day and in beautiful weather took off and headed east. I was pleasantly surprised to find myself over the castle in just twenty minutes, so took my time getting some good photos. However, on turning west to return to Redhill, I realised my stupid mistake. Although the wind was calm at ground level, at two thousand feet it was very much stronger – hence my early arrival. To return, I had to fly straight into it. With seventy-five knots indicated on the speedometer, I was only making half of this over the ground. Indeed, the cars in the country lanes below me were going much faster! The fuel tank in a Tiger Moth is located between the two upper wings, and the fuel gauge is a simple cork

The RAF trainer Chipmunks were great to learn on

Ready for take-off in the Tiger Club's famous G-ACDC, Redhill, 1968.

floating in the petrol with a wire sticking up from it. As the fuel is consumed, the wire disappears downwards. A quick glance told me that the strong headwind meant I was at serious risk of running out of fuel before reaching Redhill.

I had practised forced landings many times in the RAF. With lots of open fields below me, I was not frightened of having to attempt one for real, but the ignominy of damaging such a precious plane was too awful to contemplate. I decided to expend a little extra fuel by climbing to three thousand feet, partially hoping that the wind might be less strong, but also to give me a little more time to pick a field for an emergency landing if the engine stopped. I was lucky, and soon the grass airfield at Redhill came into sight. The wire had disappeared on the fuel gauge, meaning it was effectively empty, but relying on an element of parallax, I thought I was going to make it. With a tight circuit I landed and taxied in. Just as I rolled onto the hard apron in front of the hangar, and literally only a few yards from the refuelling point, the engine died. The refuelling engineer who had to help me push ACDC to the pumps did not mince his words about my airmanship. All in all, an experience that I shall never forget, and naturally one from which I learnt a very important lesson.

I was not frightened that day, only humiliated, but there have been two occasions on which I have managed to frighten myself. One day early in my RAF training I was practising an aerobatics manoeuvre called a stall turn. This was developed in the First World War as a way of quickly reversing direction. In the Chipmunk, you dive to gain a speed of a hundred and twenty knots then pull up in a vertical climb until the speed drops off to about fifty knots. By pushing the rudder fully to one side and the control column into your knee on the opposite side, you cartwheel to the left or right and enter a steep dive in the opposite direction to where you started. One day, I let the speed fall to almost zero and the plane went into a tailspin. Aeroplanes are not designed to fly backwards, but here I was, rushing earthwards tail first. The controls seemed useless. After what seemed an age but of course can only have been a few seconds, the aircraft flipped onto its back and I completed a sort of loop. Exciting it may have been, but it was some time before I went back to stall turns.

The other episode that challenged me in a Chipmunk was when I got too close to a thunderstorm and was directly hit by lightning. There was a very large bump and I realised that all the electrical instruments were out, including the radio. To land, you only really need the speedometer and altimeter – neither of which require electricity – to know your speed and height and I made an uneventful landing, but my pulse was racing!

Most of the flights you undertake in light aircraft are short local ones and I have been so fortunate that, living in Scotland, even short sorties from Edinburgh Airport can take you over breathtaking landscapes.

Reviewing my logbook, I realise that I have flown fourteen different types of single-engine aircraft and some of the flights have been more adventurous than my normal ones in Scotland. I will briefly recollect a few of the more unusual ones here:

Israel: In November 1993 while I was in Jerusalem for a cancer congress, I got the chance to fly the Ferrari of all single-engine light aircraft – a Mooney M20. My friend Robin Pegna introduced me to Alex Sacharov, a close friend of his who owned one of these magnificent machines and offered me a day's flying out of the small airfield in Jerusalem. With a retractable undercarriage and variable pitch propeller, this was the most sophisticated aeroplane that I had ever flown. Alex was an excellent instructor. With me in the right-hand seat and my wife Ann behind, we took off and flew north over Jericho and along the river Jordan to the Sea of Galilee. In the RAF, we were taught that when navigating by following a line-feature such as a railway line or river, you keep it to the left-hand side of the aeroplane. Sitting in the right-hand seat, the effect of parallax meant that as I followed the river, I was actually some five miles east of our planned track and, as Alex politely pointed out, probably flying in Jordanian airspace – without permission. Not a good idea. A quick left turn put me back on the west side of the river and safe from inspection by the Jordanian Air Force.

It was a truly biblical day – we flew over the Sea of Galilee and then turned south-west over Nazareth to Herzliya, a small airfield just north of Tel Aviv, where we landed for a wonderful lunch with the Sacharov family. In the afternoon it was a short flight back to Jerusalem. Sadly, there are very few Mooneys in the UK and I have not flown another since, but it was a privilege to have had at least this one experience of a truly wonderful aeroplane.

Kenya: In August 1996, Ann and I went on a safari to the Masai Mara in Kenya. En route, we planned a couple of days near Lake Naivasha, which forms part of the Great Rift Valley. On arriving at the lodge, our host asked if we had any special requests and, having noticed a windsock on the dirt airstrip nearby, I explained my passion for flying. 'Oh, Angus would be delighted to show you around,' said our host. Two hours later, I was in the co-pilot's seat of Angus's splendid, if rather old, Cessna Skylane, with Ann and his wife in the back. Ann took some wonderful photographs of our flight over Lake Nakuru with its huge flocks of pink flamingos, and we actually flew down into the crater of a huge volcano. On return I had to zoom low over the airstrip before circuiting to land to make sure that there were no lions or other large animals on the landing strip. Ann is a wonderful pilot's pal on these more adventurous trips, good at map reading and an excellent photographer.

Italy – The Alps: For many years we have gone to the French Alps to ski in Meribel, which has a very short and exciting altiport. At 1,700 metres above sea level, the runway is only 400 metres long and on an incline. Whatever the wind direction, you take off downhill and land like a duck on the uphill incline. I have flown several times at Meribel, in a wooden Jodel D140, a type of which, fortunately, I had had previous experience in the Redhill Tiger Club. However, flying off snow with skis instead of wheels takes a bit of getting used to. There are, of course, no brakes on a ski-shod aeroplane, so doing a customary engine run up before take-off means already using up some of the already short runway. Our most memorable flight was on a brilliantly clear day in February 2004. We had planned to fly around Mont Blanc, but my guide Frederic suggested that we try to fly right over the summit. With the mixture leaned right back and no oxygen for pilots or passenger we made it to 16,000 feet – the highest I have ever been in a light aircraft. Ann's photos are remarkable, as was my rather hard landing, but what a trip!

En route for Mont Blanc in a wooden Jodel. Meribel, 2004

South Africa: In November 2004 Ann and I enjoyed a wonderful trip to South Africa. From Cape Town we drove along the Garden Route and then into the wine country at Stellenbosch. En route to the latter, I spotted a windsock, and we introduced ourselves to some delightful people at the Stellenbosch Flying Club. They had an astonishing number of vintage and modern aircraft and the following day I was checked out in a four-seater Cessna Cardinal. We flew over Cape Town, round Table Mountain and then over the sea to Robben Island where Nelson Mandela had been imprisoned for eighteen years. A memorable flight. I would love to return to Stellenbosch one day.

The Hebrides: In May 2006 I decided to try some more adventurous flying in Scotland. With a pilot friend from the Edinburgh Flying Club, we booked out the club's Piper Archer for three days and headed north for the Outer Hebrides. After refuelling at Oban, we spent the first night at Plockton, which has a small airfield but with an asphalt runway that is rather short at less than 600 metres.

In excellent weather the following morning we donned full immersion wet suits and flew over the island of Skye to Benbecula, where the airfield played an important role in the Second World War. From there we headed out over the sea again to Tiree, another very bleak island; back to Oban for the night and then a magical return to Edinburgh the following day, circling Mull, flying over Jura to Gigha and Loch Lomond.

Devon: On these longer navigational trips it is a great advantage to have two pilots – one does the flying, and the other is free to monitor the navigation and operate the radio. In May 2016 my friend Malcolm Spaven and I decided to take a few days off and fly to Devon and Cornwall, where there are several small and interesting airfields. Sadly, the Edinburgh Flying Club was being wound up due to a huge increase in commercial flying at Turnhouse: our 'sewing machines' – as someone once called our single-engine aircraft – were just a nuisance to

Gigha, 2019. To land, you have to phone the day before to ask the farmer to move the sheep off the grass runway.

Air Traffic Control. In consequence the club had sold its ageing Piper Archer to an engineering company at Prestwick. While it was awaiting a major refit, we were allowed to hire 'Golf Tango' at half the usual rate. This was irresistible, so on a sunny and calm May morning we took off and headed south, planning to fly via Liverpool to Hereford and on to Dunkeswell in Devon. We knew that one of the two navigational aids was not working but as usual I had planned the route with pencil, ruler and slide rule, much to Malcolm's amusement. However, it turned out to be a good job that I had done so. I was flying the first sector, and as Blackpool Tower came into view, I asked Malcolm to switch navigation frequency to the Liverpool coordinates. As he turned the NAV button, he let out a shriek. It was red-hot! Now just about the worst thing that can happen in a small aircraft is fire. Knowing this, Malcolm managed to switch off the VOR (a navigation system which uses ground beacons to keep pilots on course), and we were both relieved that fire seemed unlikely. I was not troubled about the loss of both our navigational aids since I knew exactly where we were. However, Malcolm, a believer in all sorts of modern gadgets, then produced from his pocket a recently-bought new gizmo about the size of a mobile phone, intending to report our exact position. With a not repeatable exclamation, he announced that his new expensive toy thought that we were overhead Heathrow airport at 38,000 feet. We found Hereford by lunchtime and by late afternoon had passed over the Bristol Channel to Dunkeswell, a delightful aerodrome northeast of Exeter. I made Malcolm pay for the beers that evening out of respect for my old-fashioned but reliable navigational techniques.

The following day we had planned a series of airfield-hopping flights over Devon and Cornwall, but by breakfast time it was clear that the weather was deteriorating with a low-pressure system coming in from the east. Fearing that we might get stuck for a few days, we decided to head north and return to Scotland. I flew the first leg, back over the Bristol Channel to Cardiff and then north-west over the Cambrian Mountains to Aberystwyth and into the military zone of RAF Valley, where we landed at Caernarfon. After refuelling and a very quick lunch, we became aware that the weather due north of us was getting worse, so we decided to fly over to the Isle of Man and then northeast back to Prestwick. Flying over the sea, one normally aims for an altitude of at least 5,000 feet, both for better vision and safety, but on this occasion, we could barely make 2,000 feet. Flying over water and with no navigational aids, it is sometimes a challenge to distinguish sea from sky, but Malcolm flew very well (he is a qualified instructor) and, having explained our instrument problem, I had secured low-level radar surveillance from the RAF. From Douglas on the Isle of Man the visibility improved, and we had an uneventful flight back to Prestwick. That night I bought the beers!

These trips are just some of the happy recollections that I have from browsing my logbook. Flying has been, and still is, an immensely rewarding pastime and I realise how fortunate I was to be taught so well in the RAF at Cambridge and, in the years since, to have had the opportunity to fly some wonderful aeroplanes, especially G-ACDC. Perhaps one day I will get back to Stellenbosch – they had a whole hangar full of unusual aircraft just waiting to be flown!

6. MY MUSICAL LIFE

Apart my family, nothing in my life has been more important to me than music. It is an essential part of my life, and has been, and always will be a source of enjoyment, inspiration, comfort, relaxation and energy. I do not find it easy to put into words what music means to me, since it is its own language, and at least for me not easily translatable, but I will reflect on some aspects of my life where music has been central and indulge in recollecting some of the wonderful experiences that I have enjoyed – especially through singing. Music was a golden thread running through my schooldays and time at Cambridge. At my prep school the head of music, Miss McCleary, encouraged as many pupils as possible to engage in some musical activity. Hence in addition to starting on the piano, I learnt to play the recorder and the violin, and to sing – both in small choirs and on my own.

As I have already mentioned, my brother Robert was a child prodigy on the piano. In the days before CDs, Radio 3, Classic FM and media music, our home constantly resounded to him playing Liszt, Chopin, and Beethoven. Because the music room was constantly occupied, when I started learning to play the violin

I often had to practise in the garden. In hindsight, I pity the neighbours.

During those early years, learning to play the violin was something of a chore. My elderly teacher was not very inspiring, but she did get me up to a level where I won a music bursary to Bryanston, and because of her I was given an excellent violin. When it was time to have a full-sized instrument, she introduced my father to Clifford Hoing, a violin-maker in High Wycombe, and he made me the wonderful instrument that is now in the hands of my daughter Sarah. It has a firm but sonorous tone, well-suited to both solo and orchestral music. When I went to Bryanston, I was fortunate to be taught by Peter Chamberlain, an accomplished violinist. At the end of my first year, I had a musical epiphany when I bought my first classical music record, French violinist Christian Ferras playing the Mendelssohn Violin Concerto. I was captivated and remember playing this record over and over again all through the summer holidays. This transformed my attitude to practice and really made me want to improve my playing. I still have this record somewhere in the attic! There was a rich musical life at Bryanston in the early 1960s with frequent concerts, both informal and formal. The famous violinist Simon Standage had only just left when I arrived, and he returned several times to play with our orchestra. Both John Eliot Gardiner and Mark Elder overlapped with me at Bryanston and now, both knighted and world-famous conductors, have remained good friends. I enjoyed playing chamber music and being in the school orchestra, where I ended up on the first 'desk' next to Peter Chamberlain. When I went to Cambridge, I played

Robert was always on the piano so I had to practise my violin in the garden

for a while in the University String Players (a chamber group established by John Eliot Gardiner) and for two years led the Trinity College Orchestra. The latter was more ambitious than talented but my diary of those days records concerts where we gave some rendering of works such as Tchaikovsky's Fifth, Beethoven's Second and Dvorak's Eighth amongst others.

But my greatest enjoyment musically has come from singing. As a boy treble in my first year at Bryanston, I was paired for some duets with John Eliot, when the future world-famous founder of the Monteverdi Choir (about which I will write later) was a young tenor two years my senior. After my voice broke at the age of fourteen, it eventually settled to a useful low bass, and my tutor thought that, with formal tuition I might have a chance of a choral scholarship to Cambridge. I started singing lessons and gained valuable experience, singing solos in church, in concerts, and with the school madrigal group. The latter was conducted by the school chaplain, Pat Magee – himself an ex-King's College Cambridge choral scholar. He was great fun and, needing girls for this type of singing, would regularly drive us over to our sister school, Cranborne Chase, for evening rehearsals which would often involve stopping in a pub on the way home for what he referred to as 'barley tea'. Not all of our music was classical and in addition to madrigals, Pat Magee encouraged us to sing barber-shop close harmony songs, especially from the famous *Yale Song Book*. This light-hearted music was tremendous fun to perform and went down well as interludes during school concerts. I also learnt to play the tenor saxophone, having purchased a rather elderly instrument on Charing Cross Road. I never became very accomplished, but with some rather better jazz musician friends we formed the Stour Valley Stompers and even made a rather awful record.

In my last term at Bryanston, I went up to Cambridge, where I won a choral exhibition to Trinity College, whose musical director was Raymond Leppard. In the mid-1960s Ray Leppard, as we knew him, was at the top of his performing career. A brilliant harpsichord player, he was most famous as a conductor and I remember him inviting some of the college choir to Glyndebourne when he was conducting there. We learnt so much music from him.

One of my greatest good fortunes during my time at Cambridge was to have singing lessons from John Carol Case. His baritone voice was much in demand on the international concert stage, so I was lucky that he made time for teaching. His were certainly the best music lessons I ever had. He transformed my voice, helping me to gain much greater resonance throughout my vocal range and the breathing technique to sustain it.

The realisation that I had what they call a 'useful instrument', and the advent of the Monteverdi Choir, were an essential part of my uncertainty about whether or not to risk music as a career. Although I decided on the more reliable choice of medicine, I have been incredibly fortunate to have had the opportunity of singing at a professional level throughout my medical life. I owe this in part to the generosity of my academic colleagues in Edinburgh in allowing me time off, but most of all to John Eliot Gardiner, who has been a friend for over sixty years.

Although we had known each other briefly at

Bryanston, it was a chance meeting on King's Parade during my first term in Cambridge that set me on the path of an amazing musical journey with the Monteverdi Choir, with whom I sang for the next half-century. In the spring of 1964, John Eliot had gathered the choral scholars from King's, John's, Trinity and Clare colleges to perform a version of Claudio Monteverdi's *Vespers of 1610* in King's College Chapel. He had taken a year off from his undergraduate studies at King's to realise his own version of the *Vespers* – now well-known to audiences all over the world, but very unfamiliar in 1964. The performance was an astonishing success, and in November he decided to gather the same singers for a concert in Great St Mary's Church in Cambridge on 18 January 1965. This was the first time that we took the name 'The Monteverdi Choir'. I remember this concert for two reasons – firstly, I had never sung with such an amazingly talented group of musicians; and secondly, it was the one and only time that I heard live the astonishing voice of the tenor, Wilfred Brown. I do not think that anyone could surpass Brown for his ability to sing in English. Unlike German or Italian, English diction is not easy vocally, but Brown's recording of Finzi's *Dies Natalis* is one of my 'Desert Island Discs'. That particular piece of music is a sublime setting of poems by Thomas Traherne which I love in its own right, but Brown's diction and phrasing are for me the finest singing of its kind I have ever heard.

When he left Cambridge, John Eliot went to Paris to study with Nadia Boulanger, but back in London he wanted to regroup and develop the Monteverdi Choir. Coming down from Cambridge, some of us who had sung with him before were pursuing professional careers

*The Monteverdi Choir rehearsing in Westminster Cathedral for a Prom in 1975.
JFS is top right.*

outside music, and others were starting their careers as musicians. (The original King's Singers were all part of the early Monteverdi Choir.) For my part, I greatly welcomed the opportunity of singing again in such superb company but realised that there were other opportunities as well.

For the next few years in London, I sang with a small group called The Elizabethan Singers. Their conductor was Herrick Bunney, the organist of St Giles' Cathedral in Edinburgh, who would travel to London every Wednesday to teach at the Royal College of Organists during the day and rehearse us in the evening. Several of my friends from Cambridge, including my then partner Dorothy, were also members, and we enjoyed putting on concerts around London – especially on the South Bank – and making several recordings. In autumn 1969, we gave a concert in the Church of the Ascension in Blackheath in the autumn of 1969 to celebrate Dr John Robinson's retirement as the Bishop of Woolwich, from where he went to be Dean of Trinity College, Cambridge. In it, we gave the first performance of the *Requiem for the Living* composed by Donald Swann to wonderful words by Cecil Day Lewis. The music was challenging but it was fun meeting Swann, who was every bit as amusing in person as he was known to be on the stage. It turned out that he was also one of Herrick's great friends.

For the first few years in Edinburgh, I sang for Herrick in the St Giles' Cathedral Choir and in a group that he called the St Matthew Singers, who put on annual performances of Bach's *St Matthew Passion* in the Queen's Hall. Herrick was a brilliant organist but not a great conductor and, despite some excellent voices, these performances lacked precision and accuracy – the very qualities I so appreciated in the Monteverdi Choir. However, we became good friends, and I was thrilled when he agreed to play at my wedding in St Giles' in 1995. Sadly, two years later he died from cancer. The last time I saw him, he was an in-patient in one of our oncology wards at the Western General Hospital. I visited him at the end of the afternoon, still in my white coat. Herrick produced a bottle of whisky from his bedside table and insisted that I share a dram with him. Selfishly, I was concerned about what anyone observing would think of the professor drinking on duty, but it was typical of Herrick's generosity, and it would have been unkind to refuse.

Thinking back to my time in London, the other group that I enjoyed singing with was the choir formed in 1975 to accompany Neville Marriner's Academy of St Martin in the Fields. This chamber orchestra was then recognised as one of the foremost in Europe, but Neville had never ventured into choral work. With the help of his Hungarian friend, Lásló Heltay, he assembled quite a large choir (fifteen basses), who would rehearse under Lásló and perform with Neville. Our first performances were of Bach's B minor Mass, with which we toured in Germany in January 1975. I particularly remember singing in the Berlin Philharmonie, a magnificent concert hall with excellent acoustics.

Touring was such fun. Allowing oneself to become immersed in the music for a few days was a wonderful change from my life as a doctor. I was occasionally asked to tend the sick, however, and I remember on this German tour having to administer to our tenor soloist, the famous Robert Tear, when he developed a sore throat. What a pair of tonsils!

In those days, I used to keep press cuttings, and it was rewarding after our Berlin performance to find that the leading German music critic of the day, HH Stuckenschmidt, had written that 'he had never in his life heard such choral perfection'. We made our London debut with a performance of the Mozart Requiem in the Royal Albert Hall, a much more challenging venue acoustically. The last time I sang with this group was in the summer of 1977, when we performed Bach's B minor Mass again, but this time in the Church of St Martin-in-the-Fields itself. On this occasion, the tenor soloist was Anthony Rolfe Johnson, who became one of the finest ever exponents of Bach's evangelical roles and performed many times with John Eliot Gardiner and the Monteverdi Choir.

Much as I enjoyed and learnt a great deal from singing in The Elizabethan Singers and the Chorus of the Academy of St Martin in the Fields, nothing could match the demands and rewards of singing for John Eliot in our developing Monteverdi Choir. In 1968 we performed the *Vespers* at a Promenade Concert in the Royal Albert Hall. At twenty-five, John Eliot was the youngest conductor to ever appear in the Proms, but the packed audience loved it. We were truly on our way. Over the next decades, I was fortunate to sing in so many wonderful concert halls and cathedrals, all over Europe and in the USA, and experience the joy of performing at the very highest level. One of the exhilarations of singing is the sheer physical energy required. One's emotional response to the music is a key component of learning and rehearsal, but when it comes to performance your emotions must be controlled. Not everyone appreciates the physical demands required in singing works such as a full oratorio. Many a time when leaving a concert platform with sweat soaking through to my coat-tails I have sensed a truly pleasurable exhaustion that reminds me of finishing a winning game of rugby or a rowing race. John Eliot is a perfectionist, and we were constantly driven to achieve higher and higher levels of musical ensemble, articulation, rhythm, and diction ('Austrian' German when in Vienna, for example). The choir developed into what by 2013 was reported in the press as 'the best chamber choir in the world', and certainly to this day is still recognised as world-class.

I could go on and on, but instead I will simply reflect on a few of the more memorable concerts and recordings of my many years singing for John Eliot. I hope that this gives some flavour of my musical career.

Strasbourg, 1971: Our first European tour was to Germany and France. I have particular memories of the final concert in the magnificent cathedral in Strasbourg, since unexpectedly I had to sing the second bass part alone. We were a small choir with just four basses – two first and two second, the latter being Terry Edwards and me. The two of us were amongst the few people in London at that time who could sing down to a low D in public and we were often paired together when early Baroque music required demanded hitting such a low note. Terry went on to have a distinguished career as the chorus master at the Royal Opera House in Covent Garden. On the day of this last concert, he phoned my room after breakfast to say that he was not well, and I would be on my own that evening. Fortunately, I knew the music well since we had performed the same programme several times during the tour, but I was nervous all the same. Happily, my voice did not let me down, and I almost enjoyed the experience. I will always remember how, as we processed out down the long nave at the end of the concert, all 2,000 people in the audience stood in silence to acknowledge us. This was before the days when audiences applauded in churches, and it was incredibly moving. There was hardly a dry eye in the dressing room afterwards. All in all, a very special occasion.

The Queen Elizabeth Hall, 1972: In 1972 John Eliot gave me my first opportunity to sing solo with

Appropriately nervous in the Green Room

the Monteverdi Choir. We sang Stravinsky's *Les Noces*, a choral ballet, in the Queen Elizabeth Hall. It was recorded by the BBC, where we rehearsed beforehand. Several years later, I happened to hear a replay on the radio, and the introducer named me as 'John Smyth – basso profundo'. I rather liked that.

During the 1970s and 1980s, the reputation of the choir developed, and we made many CD recordings. I always enjoyed the sessions at the Abbey Road studios, which of course were purpose-built, but when we used churches there was a constant challenge of extraneous noise. Many of these sessions were held in the evening, and whereas live performance is accompanied by the flow of adrenaline that gives energy, multiple repeats of the same music during recording sessions at the end of a long day could be very demanding – especially if you think that you have got the right 'take' only to hear an ambulance siren or the rumble of an underground train. Certainly, the life of a professional musician is not all glamour! I remember particular frustrations while recording Monteverdi and Gabrieli motets in London's Kingsway Hall in 1972 and the *Vespers* in St Jude on the Hill in Hampstead Garden Suburb in 1974, but with John's customary aim for perfection, the CD that I still have of these is more than an excellent reward for the endeavour involved.

La Scala, 1990: The Brahms Requiem has held a special place in my musical memory since my schooldays. When I was fourteen my voice broke, and from having a useful treble voice I then, for six months or more, found it impossible to pitch notes at all. It was awful. I obviously could not continue in the school church choir, but I will never forget one Sunday morning when they sang the Brahms Requiem chorus 'How lovely are thy dwellings' (*Wie Lieblich Sind Deine Wohnungen*). I had never heard this before, but I thought that it was one of the most beautiful pieces of music I had ever come across – and I was not able to join in. I wept silently at the back of the church. Thirty years later, I sang in the Monteverdi Choir recording that we made for Phillips in St Jude's church but, more amazingly, performed from the stage of La Scala, Milan. When I requested study leave from the medical school at Edinburgh to do this tour, the dean announced at a faculty meeting that as far as records showed, I was the only professor of medicine in the university's 400-year history to ask permission to sing at La Scala. I still remember this performance and have kept the very elaborate programme. The stage at La Scala is very steeply raked, so you get an excellent view of the conductor, and the acoustic is wonderful, with surprisingly little difference in the sound between rehearsing in an empty house and performing in front of a packed audience in the actual concert. A day that I shall never forget, and the Brahms Requiem is another of my 'Desert Island Discs'.

Covent Garden, 1993: To celebrate the 250th anniversary of the first performance in London of Handel's *Messiah*, choirs and musical societies all over the UK were encouraged to put on performances of this great masterpiece in concert halls, village halls and churches all over the country on the same day. Handel had conducted the first London performance in Covent Garden, on the site of the present Opera House, and the BBC asked the Monteverdi Choir and Orchestra to perform *Messiah* from there. They broadcast it live, and it was a terrific occasion.

Well-known as it is, the *Messiah* is actually very difficult to perform to John Eliot's exacting standards. To get all eight basses to sing every hemidemisemiquaver in exactly the right place at the right time with uniform diction is quite a challenge. And as with Brahms's Requiem so with Handel's *Messiah*: modern audiences are used to much larger forces then the Monteverdi Choir. With its small numbers, the contribution of every singer is more demanding and exposed, but it is possible to achieve much greater precision in rhythm, diction and ensemble – very rewarding for the performers and seemingly well appreciated by our audiences. The morning after the concert, my friend Andrew Lister, the professor of medical oncology at St Bartholomew's Hospital, phoned me to say that he had been in a box within two metres of me on the stage and, try as he did, he was unable to distract me throughout the whole event. I explained the concentration required – especially in such awesome musical company.

The Musikverein, Vienna, 1996: The Musikverein in Vienna is the home of the world-famous Vienna Philharmonic Orchestra. In June 1996 I had one of the most wonderful musical experiences of my life when we spent a week in this amazing concert hall, singing Bruckner's First Mass with them. As an orchestra they are an institution, and I remember being surprised by the formality of the orchestra members' behaviour even during rehearsal. Gowned technicians laid out their instruments for the players, and even rosined the bows for the double bassists. The Musikverein hall – familiar as the venue for the televised New Year's Day concerts – has a wonderful acoustic, and we played each day to packed, very appreciative audiences. I also had time to explore parts of Vienna, a city with unique musical heritage, and it has become one of my favourite destinations. On a subsequent visit I chanced upon what has become one of my favourite hotels in the world, the König Von Ungarn, Vienna's oldest hotel, founded in 1746. Very close to St Stephen's Cathedral, its walls back onto the house where Mozart lived. Sleeping in its rooms, you can just about imagine him working away next door.

Salzburg, 1997: In August we performed at the Salzburg Festival, an awesome venue where even for matinee performances the audiences were dressed to the nines. We sang a piece that was new to me, but which has subsequently become another of my 'Desert Island Discs' – Schubert's setting of Goethe's poem '*Gesang der Geister über den Wasser*' (Song of the Spirits over Waters), a part song set for male voices accompanied by the low strings of the orchestra. The fast passages are so difficult for a low bass voice that I had to learn it by heart, as I couldn't follow both the manuscript and John's conducting at the same time. We were accompanied by the Vienna Philharmonic Orchestra and the concert was captured live by Deutsche Grammophon. I still have the CD. A few years later, I remember driving back to Edinburgh from a salmon fishing trip in the North of Scotland listening as it was played on Radio 3. At the end, the announcer, reading the programme notes, said, 'This claims to be from a live concert at the Salzburg Festival but surely such excellence and virtuosity could only be achieved in a recording studio.' Wrong: it was live, but with everyone on top form, no repeats were needed.

A few weeks later we performed this with our own string players at a Promenade Concert in the Royal Albert Hall in London, and I was very pleased that my daughters Sarah and Anna were in the audience. I particularly remember the virtuoso playing of our lead double bass player, Valerie Botwright. The challenging agility required from our bass voices was as nothing compared with Valerie flashing over the same notes as though she were playing a viola not a double bass. The programme ended with us performing Beethoven's Ninth, for which subsequent events have given me a special affection.

With the exception of two special concerts, for the last ten years of my time with the Monteverdi I was 'on the bench' as a reserve. Quite rightly, places were given to younger singers, but all the same I have been fortunate that, despite not having sung every week of my life, my voice has held up well over the years. I was always flattered when the 'fixer' rang to invite me to replace someone unable to sing – usually at short notice. On one such occasion I was asked if I was free for two performances of Beethoven's Choral Symphony. There were two weeks to go (but no scheduled rehearsals), but I knew the piece and thought there should be no problem. Then came the bombshell: we were required to sing it 'off copy' – in other words, by memory. The last movement of Beethoven's Ninth is only twelve minutes long but, not speaking German, I had to learn this phonetically. Of course, I had a translation and knew what the words meant and have sung a great deal in German. Pronunciation was not a problem but memorising those twelve minutes was a real challenge. For the first concert in Birmingham, I made one mistake – a dramatic solo entry one bar too soon. Fortunately, this was covered by the very loud brass section and the only person who knew was Lawrence Wallington, standing next to me, as he so often has. I had to buy him a beer after the concert to avoid being reported to John Eliot. Fortunately, I nailed it two days later in Hamburg, and all was forgiven.

The Bach Cantata Pilgrimage, 2000: This was one of the most ambitious projects ever conceived by John Eliot. By a quirk of history, the 250th anniversary of Bach's death fell in the year 2000 – an ideal moment for looking both backwards and forwards. The choir and the English Baroque Soloists undertook a mammoth year-long project to perform all 198 of Bach's surviving church cantatas on the liturgical day for which they were composed. These performances involved travel to fourteen countries in Europe, singing in some of its most beautiful churches – including ones where Bach himself performed – and ending in New York at Christmas time. All of the cantatas were recorded live and presented as a unique collection of CDs containing familiar and some unfamiliar works.

None of us could take part in all of these weekly events, and I could only join for a few. These included a concert in King's College Chapel in Cambridge (where the Monteverdi Choir started), a performance in St Mary's Church in Haddington near Edinburgh and the Marienkirche in Lübeck, where Bach studied under Buxtehude, one of the greatest organists of the day. My accountant is amused that even now – twenty years later – I still get royalties from the CDs, though the sums involved are very small.

Bach Marathon, 2013: On Easter Monday, theMonteverdi Choir staged a unique event in the Royal Albert Hall to celebrate John Eliot Gardiner's seventieth birthday. We made music all afternoon and evening, calling the whole event a 'Bach Marathon' – and it was! We started with the famous motet for double choir

'*Singet dem Herrn ein neues Lied*' – and then followed with a series of solo performances from John Eliot's friends interspersed with conversations on stage to reflect on the particular significance of some Bach masterpieces. I particularly remember the awesome Victoria Mullova, who performed another of my 'Desert Island Discs' – the Partita No2 in D minor for unaccompanied violin. It was spellbinding. In the evening we performed the Mass in B minor. I am rather chuffed that in a photo of this performance, I am the only man with grey hair. This was to be my penultimate concert with the Monteverdi Choir, but I finished on a real high.

To celebrate fifty years of the choir's existence we returned to King's College, Cambridge to perform the Monteverdi's *Vespers of 1610* on the very same calendar date to our original performance in 1964. I was one of four of the original singers to be included in that day's choir, the others being Linda Hurst, Neil Jenkins and Simon Carrington (who founded the King's Singers), all of whom have had had very distinguished singing careers. I was in extraordinary company. It was an emotional occasion for all of us 'oldies' and so many loyal supporters over the years who came to this performance and to the party afterwards. Sad as I was to realise that this was the end of singing in the choir for me, it could not have been a more fitting valediction.

So my singing days were over, but my involvement with the Monteverdi was not. John Eliot invited me to join their board of directors as a trustee, and as I write these reflections, I have just completed my six-year term in this capacity. It has been an honour and privilege to help restructure the governance of the organisation, and

The only one with grey hair! Celebrating Sir John Eliot Gardiner's 70th birthday in the Royal Albert Hall, 2013.

With Sir John Eliot Gardiner after my last performance with the Monteverdi Choir at King's College Chapel in 2014, where it had all started in 1964.

to help raise the considerable sums of money required to support their very extensive programme. One particular event that I will always treasure was the performance of the Verdi Requiem in Westminster Cathedral in September 2018. The musicians wanted to perform this magnificent work in memory of their much-loved stage manager Richard Fitzgerald, who had recently died of lung cancer. I persuaded the board that we could share the profits from this concert with Cancer Research UK, the UK's largest cancer charity. This was not only to support cancer research but allowed me, with support from Sir Paul Nurse, director of the Crick Institute, and others from the charity, to reach out to a wide range of people not previously familiar with the Monteverdi. It was a spectacular event.

Sir John Eliot Gardiner: I owe an enormous debt of gratitude to John Eliot for all the opportunities that he has given me to make music in such wonderful company as the singers and players of the Monteverdi Choir and Orchestras. To be allowed to sing with some of the best in the world, and for so many years, and in so many amazing places, has been a huge privilege. It has brought me great joy, profoundly enriched my knowledge and appreciation of music, and brought friendships that I shall always treasure. Throughout this journey, he has been my musical lodestone, and I have greatly valued our enduring friendship.

The life of a conductor can be lonely. On the concert platform and in rehearsal, they are on their own, and being the boss can be difficult in terms of friendships, as I know from my own experience as director of a large cancer research centre. When people's careers depend on you, some friendships can be insecure or even sycophantic, and lasting friendships sadly rare. Both John Eliot and I were fortunate that I never depended on him employing me to sing. I think that our mutual respect for each other professionally has been a key factor in being friends for such a long time.

Reviewing John Eliot's biography of *Bach, Music in the Castle of Heaven*, Amanda Foreman calls it 'a unique portrait of one of the greatest musical geniuses of all time by one of the greatest musical geniuses of our own age'. High praise indeed, but fully deserved. Some years ago, a journalist wrote that 'if there were a Nobel Prize for music, surely the Monteverdi Choir would be the first recipients', but of course that should go to John Eliot. His knowledge of music and especially the history of music is phenomenal, and many of us have commented on the experience of a first rehearsal when, before we had sung a note, he would introduce the work that we were preparing by recounting where the music sat in the composer's life, where it was first performed, and why it was special. No other conductor for whom I have sung has ever done this with such enthralling understanding. Another aspect of John Eliot's approach that has greatly influenced my professional life in medicine is his constant, insistent striving for excellence. He has enormous energy and on so many occasions would drive us on in rehearsal to near-exhaustion – but the results would pay off in performance. There have been many occasions where I have had to struggle with professional fatigue: preparing for an international conference, for example, taking early morning flights, dealing with noisy hotels or difficult colleagues. When I have thought about John Eliot's attitude to such challenges, I have drawn strength from the example that he has shown. The advantage that he has over me is that achieving a superb performance is a lot more rewarding than presenting at a medical conference – whatever the importance of the occasion.

I have kept several of the letters that John Eliot has written to me over the years. He liked my voice, my musicianship and especially my attitude – in rehearsal, on tour, recording or performing. We have also shared personal griefs and troubling times as well as all the highs of performance at such a high level. I shall always value his friendship and reflect on the extraordinary fortune of making wonderful music with him over so many years.

My Desert Island Discs: In one of Britain's longest-running radio programmes, an interviewee is imagined marooned on a desert island with the magical possibility of playing recorded music. In recounting their life story, he or she has to choose just eight records which would sustain them as memories of special people or events in their lives. Having enjoyed so much music in my life, both listening and performing, choosing a mere eight records would be almost impossible for me. If pushed, though, these ones mean the most:

> 1. Mendelssohn's Violin Concerto. The first piece of classical music that I listened to, in raptures, at the age of fourteen. Saturated with my brother's renderings of Liszt, Beethoven, and Chopin on the piano, this was the first music that awakened me to the awesome possibilities of the violin, and radically changed my attitude to practising.

2. Schumann's Piano Concerto. My brother Robert played this to great acclaim as his swansong before leaving school, and it always reminds me of him and his precocious talent.

3. Tchaikovsky's Sixth Symphony. The '*Pathétique*', as it is known, is a powerful work that I love in its own right. It was one of the few pieces of classical music that my father knew and really enjoyed. He would often listen to it when he was on his own, and it would remind me of him and his troubled life.

4. The Chaconne from Bach's Partita for solo violin No. 2 in D minor – one of the greatest pieces of music ever written for the violin.

5. The Brahms Requiem. This wonderful work haunted me at school and brought exhilaration singing it in the Monteverdi Choir, not least at La Scala in Milan. It would remind me of all the amazing experiences I had with the choir.

6. Schubert's *Gesang der Geister über den Wassern*. This setting of a poem by Goethe sung by male voices, accompanied by the lower strings in the orchestra, was one of the most challenging pieces that I ever performed in the Monteverdi Choir. I remember singing it at the Salzburg Festival, which was recorded, and at a Prom in London. Listening to it on my desert island would remind me of the exacting discipline that John Eliot Gardiner demanded of us in musical performance and of the many lessons of life that I have learnt from seeking perfection – or at least aiming for it – in other aspects of my life as well as in music.

7. Gerald Finzi's *Dies Natalis*. This beautiful work for tenor and orchestra sets to music poems by Thomas

Traherne. The famous recording by Wilfred Brown is in my opinion near perfection for singing in the difficult language of English – his diction and phrasing is astonishing. As in my last choice, this exhibition of excellence would inspire me in my new-found solitude to remember the importance of trying one's best in all circumstances, whatever the outcome.

8.   Bach's St Matthew Passion. Perhaps the greatest piece of music ever composed? I love the bass solo which comes near the end – as Herrick Bunney described it, the 'dénouement' of the whole work – '*Mache dich, mein Herze, rein, Ich will Jesum selbst begraben. Denn er soll nunmehr in mir, Für und für….*'– 'Make me clean, my heart, from sin; I would my Lord inter. May He find rest in me, Ever in eternity.' What greater comfort could there be, alone on a desert island?

7. TRAINING

St Bartholomew's Hospital Medical College: 1967-70

I started my clinical training at St Bartholomew's Hospital London (Barts) in the autumn of 1967. The three-year course was divided up into three-month attachments to 'firms'. A firm consisted of two consultants, a team of senior and middle-grade registrars, a senior house officer and two pre-registration house officers. Typically at Barts, each firm would be responsible for a male and a female ward of twenty-five beds each, although naturally this varied for specialties such as obstetrics and gynaecology.

Compared with my later experience as a professor in Edinburgh, the clinical teaching at Barts was very loosely structured. There were relatively few lectures, no assigned tutors or directors of studies, and we were very much left to fend for ourselves. At all times we were assigned to specific wards and on most days, we would have a one-to-two-hour session led by one of the firm's doctors – either a consultant or a registrar – but the teaching was entirely dependent on which patients were available at any one time.

In my first year we spent six months on medical wards and six on surgical wards. Each firm was specialised and, in my case, the medical wards were focused on leukaemia and lymphoma, chest diseases, gastroenterology and diabetes. The surgical firms were highly specialised and included arterial surgery and the surgical management of portal hypertension. Each medical firm took it in turns to admit emergencies, and this involved patients presenting with heart attacks, acute asthma and strokes, so we did see some general medical practice. Surgery was less helpful for us students. We saw a lot of patients with minor injuries from working at Smithfield meat market, but virtually none of the common things I had to deal with as a pre-registration house officer in a district general hospital later on. I didn't, for example, see a single case of acute appendicitis in all my three years at Barts.

For the more formal aspects of our studies, we were recommended to use a well-known textbook, *Davidson's Principles and Practice of Medicine*. I did not appreciate at the time that this excellent book was written by consultants from the Western General Hospital and Royal Infirmary in Edinburgh, and was initiated in 1952 by Sir Stanley Davidson, a passionate teacher who led medicine at the Western. When I was appointed to a chair in Edinburgh, I was invited to write the first chapter on medical oncology for *Davidson's* and contributed to many subsequent editions. Several of the authors I read as a student became colleagues and personal friends.

Our second year of clinical training included psychiatry, obstetrics, gynaecology, and paediatrics. At Barts, the latter was even more specialised than medicine and surgery and was mostly devoted to children with cancer, so I asked permission to do my three months' placement in paediatrics elsewhere. I chose

Addenbrooke's Hospital, to allow me to enjoy another few months back in Cambridge. This gave me one of the best experiences of all my clinical studies. The sole consultant paediatrician at Addenbrooke's was a truly inspirational man – Dr Douglas Gairdner. When I had written some months beforehand to ask if attachment to his practice would be possible, he wrote a short, cautious reply saying yes but with no detail at all. When I arrived, I realised why. Over the years, he had had several similar requests, but no-one had ever shown up. This was their loss, because although Addenbrooke's was not at that time a teaching hospital, Dr Gairdner was a wonderful teacher. For three months he allowed me to follow him around, five to six days a week, on the ward or in outpatient clinics. I saw and learnt so much during that time. Douglas Gairdner had an encyclopaedic knowledge of paediatrics. He was at that time editor of the *Archives of Disease in Childhood*, but his greatest gift was his ability to communicate with children and their inevitably anxious parents. He taught me how to speak with children – a most rewarding experience that I have enjoyed ever since. Towards the end of this time, when Dr Gairdner's house officer was ill, I was allowed to be the locum. I still remember the scary opportunities of performing lumbar punctures on toddlers with suspected meningitis, putting up a scalp-vein drip to transfuse a six-month-old little boy, and my nights of monitoring children with croup. Douglas Gairdiner was one of the hardest-working doctors I have ever met. The single-handed responsibility for so many ill children was undertaken day in, day out – and he never complained. A true inspiration to me, as a result of which I seriously considered a career in paediatrics.

I never really enjoyed obstetrics. We were required to deliver fifty babies and I was glad when I reached this number – mostly on a month's secondment to Redhill Hospital. I remember two deliveries in particular. During my first month of obstetrics at Barts, it was my turn to assist a rather large Italian lady. By the time I was gowned and gloved, it was obvious that the baby was about to appear. It was good that I had played cricket in my youth because, after a huge grunt, a little baby boy literally shot out – only (just) to be caught by me. The mother, realising that I was a bit surprised, collapsed back on the pillows and, in her strong Italian accent exclaimed, 'Do not worry – he is my thirteenth!' Also at Redhill, one morning I delivered a small boy to a mother exhausted by a long and difficult labour. Relieved, she asked me what my name was and decided to call the newborn 'John'. I was flattered. That afternoon, I had time off to fly Tiger Moth G-ACDC at the nearby Tiger Club, then caught the train to London for an evening recording session with John Eliot Gardiner and the Monteverdi Choir. One of my better days.

Our exposure to general practice and psychiatry was not very inspiring, but the teaching was better in dermatology and ophthalmology. In our third year, we were allowed to do short periods as locum housemen. I realise now, in comparison to today's student training, that although the formal teaching was less organised, we did have the opportunity to carry out far more practical procedures. Thus, even before I qualified, I was able to do pleural drainage and biopsies, lumbar punctures and set up countless numbers of IV lines. The whole experience was more of an apprenticeship, learning by doing rather than following a specific course of instruction. I was fortunate to do a short locum in the firm to which I was subsequently assigned for my first pre-registration house job. Dr Anthony Dawson (later to become Sir Anthony, the Queen's physician) was a pioneer of the then new discipline of gastroenterology. He was an exceptional physician interested in the science of intestinal illness, but especially concerned with the link between the psyche and the soma. Many of his patients had inflammatory bowel disease – ulcerative colitis or Crohn's disease – where patients' mental health can closely affect their gastrointestinal function.

I learnt how to do liver biopsies and sigmoidoscopies. Towards the end of our third year, we applied for the pre-registration house jobs that were to follow once we completed our basic training. We were required to do six months of medicine and six months of surgery. Having decided to become a physician, I applied for one of only five medical house jobs at Barts and was thrilled to get my first choice – with Dr Dawson.

For our final exams, we returned to Cambridge and over a hectic three weeks we completed written and oral exams in medicine, surgery, obstetrics and all the different disciplines of the clinical curriculum. Having described the rather haphazard course at Barts I remember that these exams, concentrated as they were, brought all the different strands of our clinical studies together – and I actually enjoyed them. I passed them all and became a doctor.

Graduating as a doctor, Cambridge, 1970.

House Physician (1970-1)

In October 1970, I embarked on my pre-registration year. I was fortunate to be in familiar surroundings and well supported by registrars above me, but my major recollection is of utter exhaustion. The workload was awful. Naturally, as you gain experience you become more efficient, but those first six months were the most physically challenging of my entire career. With twenty-five beds to look after, I was on call for twice that number every other night. On alternate weeks, I had a continuous shift from Thursday morning until the next Monday evening, not only looking after my own inpatients but 'on take' for medical emergency admissions. I was lucky to get even two hours of sleep – and even that could be interrupted with phone calls. This pattern of work for junior doctors has long since been abandoned but, having survived it, I do recognise the extraordinary amount of clinical medicine that we experienced in those early years compared with current practice. Contact with Dr Dawson was limited to consultant ward rounds, but I developed the greatest respect for him. As with the paediatrician Dr Gairdner, his greatest skill was in communication. He taught us by example how to talk – and especially listen – to patients. Although he had a highly successful Harley Street private practice, he was also very interested in research and developed a large group of research workers around him, many of whom went on to populate the new specialty of gastroenterology around the country.

My six-month surgical pre-registration job was less demanding. The Royal Berkshire Hospital was a busy district general hospital in Reading, but the surgical standards were high. At last, I got to see some common surgical problems and was allowed to do a lot of minor operations and some appendectomies on my own. However, most of the time as a surgical house officer you were just admitting elective cases and holding retractors for the trained surgeons in theatre. Although the consultants and nurses were kind, this experience confirmed my choice to be a physician.

For all of us trained in London and hoping to pursue a career as a physician, the next step after registration was to try for a senior house officer post in one of the three 'glory trail' hospitals – the Royal Postgraduate Medical School at the Hammersmith Hospital, the National Hospital for Nervous Diseases at Queen Square, or the Brompton Hospital (which specialised in chest and cardiac diseases). I applied for the Hammersmith and put as my first choice the clinical pharmacology firm run by Professor Colin Dollery and his senior lecturer, Dr Alasdair Breckenridge. The large interview panel were quite scary, so I was delighted to be offered the job.

SHO at the Hammersmith (1971-2)

My six months at the Hammersmith were marred only by failing my first attempt at the Part 1 exam for membership of the Royal College of Physicians (MRCP). I foolishly put myself forward with far too little preparation. I had always found multiple-choice tests very difficult, as I could often think of more than one answer to most question. In this exam, a point was deducted for every incorrect answer, which for me made it a nightmare. Only four attempts at Part 1 were allowed, and in fact I failed a second time some six months later, so I was particularly relieved to pass on my third attempt. The second part of the exam was a proper clinical test and I passed first time. By that time, I had learnt that both Professor Dollery and my next boss, Gordon Hamilton Fairley, had had several attempts at passing the MRCP exam too, so I was in good company.

Clinical work at the Hammersmith was very different to the experience I had had in my pre-registration year, with the emphasis very much on research. I found myself the junior doctor on a truly remarkable firm. Colin Dollery was later knighted for his services to clinical pharmacology. Alasdair Breckenridge was appointed to the chair of clinical pharmacology in the subject at Liverpool University and knighted when he was chairman of the Committee on Safety of Medicines (CSM). My senior registrar was Charles George, later appointed to the chair of clinical pharmacology at Southampton University and knighted in 1998 before becoming director of the British Heart Foundation. My registrar, Michael Rawlings, was appointed the professor of clinical pharmacology in Newcastle University and knighted for his services as chairman of the CSM. Not a bad team of trainers, then, and all of them remained friends after my brief time at the Hammersmith. Alasdair Breckenridge followed my career with particular interest and invited me to be the CSM's first medical oncologist. . He spoke at my Festschrift in Edinburgh in December 2008, but sadly died of pancreatic cancer in 2019.

Training in Medical Oncology (1972-5)

Towards the end of my time at the Hammersmith, I received a phone call from St Bartholomew's Hospital asking me to go and see Professor Gordon Hamilton Fairley, who was about to be appointed Britain's first professor of medical oncology. The subject was already established in the US, but not at that time in Britain, though Fairley, who had trained in clinical haematology, had developed a special interest in the leukaemias and lymphomas. He was the first consultant at Barts to be allocated beds specifically for patients with cancer and became the founder of medical oncology in the UK, with the first professorship in the subject (at London University) funded – as mine was to be – by the Imperial Cancer Research Fund. His 'firm' was the first to which I had been sent as a first-year clinical student in 1967, and I had seen straight away what a charismatic physician he was. As with my other early medical mentors – Gairdner, Dawson, and Breckenridge – Fairley was a great communicator. He had a wonderful sense of humour and extraordinary energy. He had himself experienced cancer, having survived a testicular seminoma, and he had genuine empathy with patients.

When I went to meet him at Barts he explained that he had identified the need to train a group of young physicians in the methodology of clinical research as applied to the management of his patients with acute myeloid leukaemia (AML) and Hodgkin's disease in particular. At that time the results of treating AML were poor. Although much more successful, the treatments for Hodgkin's disease were toxic and really difficult for patients. Fairley felt that everyone should be entered into clinical trials, with careful documentation of the results. He had obtained funding for an assistant lecturer post specifically to look after his Hodgkin's patients and help with the analysis of the results of treatment. I had been recommended to him from my time as a pre-registration house officer, and he offered me this one-year post. I was, of course, flattered to be headhunted in this way, encouraged that this would give me the relative stability of a twelve-month contract, and not being full-time on the wards meant I would have some time to study for the MRCP exams. It turned out to be a life-changing experience.

I learnt so much from Gordon Hamilton Fairley. He was truly inspirational. His enthusiasm for the young science of cancer medicine, with its enormous needs and primitive tools, was infectious. His ability to use humour, even in the most demanding clinical situations, taught me lessons that I found of inestimable value later in my career. His ability to talk with and listen to dying patients was extraordinary.

His senior lecturer was another very fine physician, Derek Crowther – later the first professor of medical oncology at the Christie Hospital in Manchester. Inspired by both these men, I decided to commit to a career in the subject myself.

Every two or three weeks, Gordon used to challenge me to games of squash. Even though I was younger and (I thought) reasonably fit, he would always beat me. In fact, he had so much energy that even after the matches, striding down the corridors or taking the stairs two at a time, I would struggle to keep up. He was such a live wire that anyone would. We became friends, and when I finally passed my MRCP, he took me to dinner at his club, the Savage, in St James. Their motto is 'the pursuit of happiness' and is sometimes described as 'the leading bohemian gentlemen's club in London'. It was the first time I had ever been to such an establishment, and I remember that we had a wonderful time.

My clinical responsibility in this post involved administering the chemotherapy to patients with Hodgkin's disease. Gordon had developed a four-drug combination of nitrogen mustard, vinblastine, procarbazine and prednisolone (MVPP). The first two of these drugs had to be injected intravenously, and I remember to this day what a harrowing experience this was – for both patient and doctor. (We had clumsy reusable needles for intravenous access, completely unlike modern day 'butterflies', and no chemotherapy nurses.) Despite using the available antiemetics, these drugs caused serious nausea and vomiting. Anticipating this from their experience of previous treatments, many patients would start vomiting as I inserted the cannula. A decade later, I researched ways to improve the emesis caused by anticancer drugs by studying their clinical pharmacology and enjoyed some of the most successful research of my career.

Gordon was delighted when I decided on medical oncology as a career and encouraged me to seek funding for a research project to submit a thesis for a Doctor of Medicine (MD) degree. From my original interest in biochemistry and the experience at the Hammersmith Hospital, I decided to pursue an interest in the clinical pharmacology of anticancer drugs. In those days, very little was known about the distribution within the body and metabolism of the small number of drugs that were then available. Scientific drug development was in its infancy. Gordon introduced me to Tom Connors at the Chester Beatty Research Institute associated with the Royal Marsden Hospital. Between them, they secured for me a two-year fellowship from the Cancer Research Fund.

However, before moving to the Institute, another life-changing event took place. I got married. Cathy was a very attractive and intelligent trainee social worker, on a placement from the London School of Economics, when I met her towards the end of my time at the Hammersmith. During my year back at Barts, we had a somewhat tempestuous relationship. Cathy was keen to get married. Knowing of my reluctance to commit when I had been with Dorothy, we agreed to get married in September 1973. Cathy's father was a consultant chest physician in Gloucestershire and had trained at Barts, where he met her mother, a strong-willed Welsh nurse. They had married just after the war and had three children – a son and Cathy, who was one of a pair of identical twins. They lived in a lovely house in Cheltenham, where they held a superb reception after our wedding. We were married in the nearby Charlton Kings church with David Bruce Payne (at that time an assistant organist at Westminster Abbey) playing the organ and several friends from the Monteverdi Choir providing some wonderful singing. It was a lavish occasion, embellished with vintage cars to travel to and from the church. My parents and their family were particularly pleased that I seemed to be reconnecting with my Gloucestershire roots. That autumn I joined the department of applied biochemistry in the Institute of Cancer Laboratories in Sutton, where I stayed for the next two years. Cathy got a job at the Maudsley Hospital in Camberwell, and we decided to try to buy a house in or near Sutton. We had very little money and I cannot now remember what mortgage interest rates were, but we were very fortunate that Sutton council offered a hundred per cent mortgages on some properties and so we were able to buy our first home – a small, two-bedroom terraced cottage – and make, for the price of £10,500, a humble first step on the housing ladder.

We had a two good years there. Cathy enjoyed the Maudsley and, in addition to my laboratory project, I enrolled in an MSc programme in biochemistry run by Chelsea College, London University. This involved an afternoon and evening every Monday during term time with lectures and practicals. All the students were at the same stage in their professional development as I was, and we had a lot of fun. The exams at the end were not too challenging and I learnt a lot of general biochemistry which helped with my specific MD project.

Many projects assigned to PhD and MD students provide but one link in the chain of their supervisor's main programme, but I was fortunate to be able to embark on a new project of my own making, and one which kickstarted an international reputation in the science community for drug discovery. My attention had been drawn to an enzyme involved in purine metabolism – Adenosine Deaminase (ADA) – that appeared to have specific importance in the metabolism of lymphocytes. Some children are born with an inborn error of metabolism where this enzyme is genetically deleted. At that time, it was realised that, while normal at birth, they soon developed severe combined immunodeficiency (SCID), where all their lymphocytes disappeared, and they died of infection. All of their other systems appeared normal, and it was therefore concluded that, while protected by maternal metabolism in utero, they were unable to sustain lymphocyte numbers and function in independent life.

Nothing was known about the activity of ADA in malignant lymphocytes – leukaemias or lymphomas – so I thought it would be worthwhile to investigate. With help from senior scientists at the Institute, I learnt how to separate the white cells from whole blood, count them, disintegrate them with ultrasound and measure the ADA activity, using spectrometry that I had learnt at Great Ormond Street. I collected fresh blood cells from a range of newly diagnosed leukaemia cases and the results were fascinating. Although increased in several types of leukaemia, the ADA levels were especially raised in cases of acute lymphocytic leukaemia. I published my first paper on this in *The British Journal of Cancer* in 1975. I then posed the question of whether this increased enzyme activity was due to the need for the product of the reaction that ADA catalyses (the conversion of adenosine to inosine), or the need to reduce the levels of adenosine.

This memoir is not the place to detail scientific research, but in due course I showed that adenosine is toxic to lymphocytes, and the increased ADA activity in rapidly dividing leukaemic lymphocytes is an attempt to regulate this. I then posed the question of what would be the effect of inhibiting ADA: could this increase adenosine levels to be specifically toxic to lymphoblasts and be a useful anti-leukaemic drug? The literature had no known inhibitors of ADA, but I had another episode of great good fortune. The Institute of Cancer Research had many visitors, and one day I was introduced to a Japanese scientist who seemed interested in my project. I explained that I was searching for an inhibitor of ADA, and he recommended that I write to his boss, Professor Hameo Umezawa, at the National Institute of Health Sciences in Japan. Umezawa was an expert in deriving medicines from natural sources and, amongst other projects, had discovered Bleomycin, a compound used for treating lymphomas and other diseases. I wrote explaining my findings to date and asking for any advice he could offer. To my surprise and delight, some weeks later I received a reply enclosing a small packet of white powder labelled coformycin. To cut a long and exciting story short, with the help of expert enzymologists at the Institute, I went on to show that coformycin not only inhibited ADA at very low concentrations, but with a Ki of 10-12 molar was the most potent inhibitor of any enzyme yet described.

By this time, I was nearing the end of my two-year fellowship at the Institute and was confident that I had enough material to submit to Cambridge University for a Doctor of Medicine (MD) degree. Cathy had been very tolerant of my long days working in the lab, and even more so when I took all my notebooks with us on a camping holiday in the summer of 1975, where I wrote most of my thesis in a borrowed caravan. To finish this particular story, I was summoned to Cambridge some six months later for a viva exam on my thesis. Somewhat scarily, the senior examiner was Professor Max Perutz, who had won a Nobel Prize some ten years earlier for his determination of the structure of haemoglobin. He was kind but asked very penetrating questions and seemed genuinely interested in the originality of my work. Again, fortune smiled on me. In my reading of the existing literature on ADA at the beginning of my project I was of course aware of the link between ADA deficiency and SCID, but also that there was a tribe of people in the Kalahari Desert who had ADA deficiency but normal lymphocytes. What I had not realised was that this research had been done by none other than the man in front of me. From his breast pocket, Perutz produced an old photograph of some men from this tribe and asked if I had any idea why he was showing this to me. I got the right answer and they awarded me an MD without any corrections. Indeed, the Regius Professor of Physic, Professor Butterfield, who chaired my viva, strongly encouraged me to pursue the development of an ADA inhibitor as a new medicine for leukaemias and lymphomas.

Some months before my Cancer Research Campaign (CRC) fellowship came to an end, I had sought the advice of Gordon Hamilton Fairley as to the next steps in my career. I obviously wanted to continue developing ADA inhibitors, but I needed broader clinical experience. Gordon recommended that I go to one of the big American centres. He introduced me to Vincent De Vita, head of medicine at the National Cancer Institute (NCI), part of the National Institutes of Health (NIH) near Washington, and Joseph Bertino at Yale University. Both were founders of medical oncology in the US – Vince developed the first combination of drugs that cured Hodgkin's disease, and Jo was the discoverer of methotrexate, one of the first antimetabolites. I was offered a place by both of them and chose the NCI but I am privileged that I became friends of both over the subsequent years, and we are still in contact today – forty-five years later. Despite differences in age, there was a wonderful camaraderie amongst the early pioneers of medical oncology, and the support and friendship of people like Vince De Vita and Joseph Bertino have so much enriched my professional life over the years.

So, in the autumn of 1975, Cathy and I rented out our

little home in the UK and set off for Bethesda, Maryland, for what turned out to be one of the best years of our lives. Backed by Gordon Hamilton Fairley, I had gained a Medical Research Council travelling fellowship and the NCI was able to give me a Fogarty fellowship as well, so for the first time in our married life we were in funds. We rented a small but well-appointed apartment within walking distance of NIH and bought a seven-litre Buick Skylark – a real gas-guzzler, but petrol was so cheap that it hardly mattered.

The medical system that I joined at the National Cancer Institute was very different to that in the UK. The institute's Medicine Branch was headed by Dr Robert (Bob) C Young, since his predecessor Vince De Vita had been promoted to be clinical director. Bob was supported by five other 'attending physicians' – their equivalent of consultants. Unlike in the UK, these doctors only served on the wards and out-patients for two-month spells, two or at most three times a year. This left them time for uninterrupted research – a luxury we never attained within the UK system, either in university or NHS settings. The only downside of this arrangement was that they gained less clinical experience than our system provides. By the time I retired from clinical practice, I estimate that I had looked after more than 6,000 families with cancer during my time in Edinburgh – a wealth of experience that would be hard for anyone to match in the US. Day-to-day patient care at the NCI was the responsibility of 'clinical associates'– their equivalent of registrars. Like the Hammersmith, the NCI was a prestigious place and these 'trainees' were the pick of their various medical schools. After general medical training and obtaining their medical board exams, they spent two years at NCI and most went on to senior roles in the rapidly developing medical oncology specialty throughout the US. Two contemporaries of mine were Sam Broder and Jim Doroshow. Sam followed Vince De Vita as director of NCI and Jim has a senior leadership role there to this day.

What I gained most during my year at the National Institutes of Health was to learn the discipline of clinical research. Every patient admitted to the medicine branch had to fulfil the entry criteria for one of their ongoing protocols. Treatment was free of charge – a huge benefit in the American health system, but of course patients had to consent to their participation in research. While the Medicine Branch focused on lymphomas, Bob Young's special interest was in ovarian cancer, and he led me to develop a lifelong interest in this challenging disease. These were the days before computerised tomography (CT) scanning, so assessment of treatment response required patients to undergo keyhole laparoscopy carried out by the medical oncologists. It was also before platinum-based chemotherapy. Cisplatin was already being trialled for young men with testicular cancer, although the need for concomitant effective anti-sickness medicine was already apparent.

I saw a lot of patients with breast cancer, and at the nearby Veterans Hospital learnt how to do bronchoscopies in patients with lung cancer. A close friend of Bob Young's and one of his attending physicians was Bruce Chabner, whose special interest was clinical pharmacology. I learnt so much from these two men, and we have been friends and collaborators ever since.

After NCI, Bob was appointed Director of the Fox Chase Cancer Center in Philadelphia and has had a very distinguished career. Bruce Chabner was appointed to a chair at Harvard, where he similarly had great distinction as director of clinical research at the Cancer Centre in the Massachusetts General Hospital. Under Bob and Bruce's instruction I learnt about the rigour of NCI's approach to drug development. Following toxicity studies in animals, there were extremely cautious approaches to initial trials in patients to explore human toxicities. These were followed by trials of therapeutic efficacy and then randomised comparisons with contemporary established treatments. With such an emphasis on research, the whole environment was exciting, busy and purposeful.

My main purpose in going to the NCI was to gain clinical experience and learn the processes of clinical research that were much more advanced and disciplined than in the UK at that time. I was, however, hoping to continue my interest in ADA inhibitors from my work at the Institute of Cancer Research in London. I was in luck. When I explained my work to date with coformycin, I found out that the preclinical researchers at NCI were working with the deoxy-equivalent deoxycoformycin (DCF) similarly a potent inhibitor of ADA. They envisaged this compound as an adjunct drug to enhance the activity of adenosine analogues that were limited in their efficiency by being metabolised by ADA. On the basis of my work in London, I persuaded them to consider DCF as a unique drug in its own right. When I met Vince De Vita and explained my excitement about developing ADA inhibitors, he not only facilitated this but decided to alter his researchers' routines to allocate specific drugs to specific researchers, as in my case, to generate the enthusiasm of some 'ownership' of projects – a concept that was new to the NCI but proved very useful to them in the years ahead.

During my time at NCI, I gave my first presentation at an American Association for Cancer Research meeting, which in those days was held in the same venue with the annual American Society of Clinical Oncology. I presented my data on ADA and its inhibition, and there was considerable interest in the new approach. In consequence, I was invited to give seminars at two of America's most prestigious cancer centres – St Jude's Children's Hospital in Memphis and the MD Anderson in Houston. St Jude's was famous for the series of sequential clinical trials for children with Acute Lymphoblastic Leukaemia (ALL), conducted by Donald Pinkel, Jo Simone and Sharon Murphy. Over the years, they improved the cure rate for these children from five per cent to more than ninety-five per cent, an amazing achievement. Both St Jude's and MD Anderson wanted to develop clinical pharmacology, and I was offered positions at both hospitals. At the MD Anderson, I met Jay Freireich, another founder of American medical oncology, who with Tom Frei at the NCI had worked successfully on new treatments for ALL. Jay was very interested in my work with the coformycins and offered me a senior post to develop this in collaboration with his laboratory led by Ti Li Loo. He wanted to challenge the bureaucracy surrounding 'first into man' studies and envied the greater flexibility that I could take advantage of on my return to the UK. Flattered as I was by all these job offers, I had decided to return to the Royal

Marsden for many reasons, but two in particular. The first was an appalling tragedy. One afternoon in October 1975 my father telephoned me from London to tell me that Gordon Hamilton Fairley had been killed by an IRA terrorist bomb. He'd been out walking his dogs when one of them triggered the explosion of a bomb planted under the car of his neighbour, a prominent politician who had been the intended target. Gordon was killed instantly. He was forty-five. Apart from the sadness of losing him in such a hideous way, our small cadre of medical oncologists in London was thrown into shock. Gordon was a unique leader, and so many plans for the specialty had been influenced by him.

The second event was an invitation from the head of medicine at the Royal Marsden, Professor Phil Bondy, to be his senior lecturer when my time at NCI was over. Despite my excitement at the American approach to oncology, I decided to return to my medical roots.

And so our time in the US came to an end. Apart from the terrible news from London, it hadn't been too bad. Cathy had obtained work with a local group of psychiatrists and we made friends with several of them, as well as with my associates at NCI. We also travelled: over the Christmas break we drove the Skylark up to Canada and skied; in the spring we flew to the West Coast and drove from San Francisco through the Mohave Desert to Las Vegas, where a lucky dollar tripped the jackpot on a slot machine resulting in flashing lights and the floor covered in coins. At the end of our stay in Bethesda we had a wonderful holiday in the Caribbean. It was a year that neither of us could ever forget.

8. CONSULTANT

Senior Lecturer at the Royal Marsden (1976-9)

In the autumn of 1976 we returned to Sutton, and I began what turned out to be a very turbulent and difficult time as a senior lecturer on the professorial unit at the Royal Marsden Hospital. For the first year my clinical status was as a senior registrar and for the second and third I was an honorary consultant.

The head of the unit, Professor Phil Bondy, was not a medical oncologist but a distinguished endocrinologist from Yale University. A short time after my return, he announced that he would resign in a year's time to return to the US. The staff at the Marsden were greatly concerned at this development. Everyone had known that Bondy would only stay for a few years, and presumed that he would be replaced by Gordon Hamilton Fairley. Now, of course, this could not happen.

Bondy's resignation unsettled the staff. The senior physician at the Marsden was Dr Tim McElwain, an excellent physician with a special interest in children with cancer. He was greatly admired by his colleagues but had had no formal training in academic medicine. I was the youngest of the senior staff but at that time probably had the best training in medical oncology of anyone in the UK. Some of my supporters wanted me to succeed Bondy but a stronger lobby hoped that McElwain would be appointed.

Despite the challenging atmosphere, I was able to achieve my primary goal of testing deoxycoformycin in man. The drug worked and we formed the nucleus of a 'first into man' unit to experiment with other novel drugs. Phil Bondy had been responsible for looking after patients with lung cancer. Taking over this practice, I set up joint clinics with colleagues from the Brompton Hospital, who had many such patients, where I was also given honorary consultant status.

The best part of those three years at Sutton was my involvement with friends in Europe through the European Organisation for Research and Treatment of Cancer – the EORTC. Before leaving the NCI, Vince De Vita had asked me to go to its headquarters in Brussels and introduce myself to Omar Yoder, his 'American ambassador' there. Already, the organisation received significant funding from the NCI, as Europe was seen as a key player in extending their evaluation of new drugs. At that time, the pharmaceutical industry played only a small part in anticancer drug development, and the NCI was the major source of novel agents. Omar, a geneticist by training, was a very friendly man, a great host and played a major role in linking together our small band of US-trained European oncologists. Heine Hansen in Copenhagen, Bob Pinedo in Amsterdam, Franco Cavalli in Lugano, Pierre Alberto and Matti Aapro in Geneva, Michel Clavel in Lyon and a small number of other friends formed the organisation's early clinical trials group to agree common protocols and to learn together how to optimise early phase drug evaluation. We would meet three or four times a year, sometimes at airports, sometimes in each other's homes. To complement the clinical trials, we founded the pharmacokinetics and metabolism group, of which I was the first chairman. I still remember hosting the first meeting of this group at my old college. Twenty or so met over a couple of days in Cambridge at Trinity's Old Combination Room. It was December and the heating had failed, so there we were in overcoats, but nevertheless a cheerful bunch, knowing that we were breaking new ground in developing the clinical pharmacology of anticancer drugs.

In the spring of 1978 adverts appeared for the both the chair of medicine at the Marsden and a new chair of medical oncology at the University of Edinburgh, funded by a generous endowment from the Imperial Cancer Research Fund. I knew all about the challenges of the chair at the Marsden funded by the Cancer Research Campaign (CRC) but nevertheless decided to apply. The process was straightforward. Three of us applied, and all were interviewed a few weeks after the closing date. I felt that my interview went well: the external assessors were interested in my research but, as expected, there were awkward questions from the internal interviewers. Later, on the day of the interview, I was informed that the committee were unable to reach a decision and decided to delay the appointment until a new director of the Institute of Cancer Research had been appointed: this was expected within a few months. I later learnt that the local members of the committee favoured Tim McElwain as expected, but the externals from the University of

London preferred me.

While this was going on, I decided to visit Edinburgh to learn more about their plans. My first concern was to sound out whether someone as young as myself (I was only thirty-two) and who was in many ways an outsider, would even be considered for such an esteemed position. Even on my first visit, though, I was hugely encouraged by the genuine enthusiasm amongst the senior members of faculty for this new development and was assured that I would not be making a fool of myself by putting in an application. There were no medical oncologists in Edinburgh at that time and indeed the initial challenge for a new professor would be to establish medical oncology both within the NHS as a platform for clinical research, and within the university as a basis for collaborative scientific research and teaching both undergraduates and, in due course, postgraduates. This was clearly a huge challenge but the generous funding and the established excellence of cancer-related scientific research in Edinburgh made the position really exciting. Where the chair at the Marsden required a new captain on the bridge to slowly redirect a large tanker, Edinburgh needed a pioneer to captain his or her own fast motorboat to reach new shores.

The only senior clinicians that I knew in Edinburgh at that time were two professors of surgery – Professor Pat Forrest, who had an international reputation for his work on breast cancer, and Professor Geoffrey Chisholm, a urologist whom I knew from my days at the Hammersmith. Sir Alistair Currie was head of the department of pathology and at that time chairman of the CRC's scientific committee. I had met him when he had chaired a five-year review at the Royal Marsden in the recent past. All three of them men warned me that part of the enthusiasm that I was witnessing was due to the levels of funding for the new post, which many people hoped could help their own (collaborative) research.

The new chair had been advertised in the spring but, to my surprise when I received a letter informing me that I was shortlisted, the interview would not take place till late November. I spent an unsettled summer, but on making several visits to Edinburgh, I found my growing ambition and enthusiasm for the new job balanced by feeling nearly certain that I wouldn't get it. However, in retrospect, the very fact that I felt it was so unlikely that I would be chosen, put me in a surprisingly calm mood when the day eventually arrived for the appointment committee, just one month after my thirty-third birthday. Eleven people had applied and they selected five of us for the interview, which I described at the start of this book.

When I found out that I'd got the job, I had, perhaps naively, assumed thought that this would settle the tensions at the Marsden, but in fact the reverse happened. On my return to London, I was summoned to the acting director's office, and offered the top job. I was genuinely confused, and surprised. My supporters in London wanted me to stay, especially my colleagues at the Brompton, but I knew leading the academic programme at the Marsden would be a huge challenge, especially overcoming opposition from the supporters of Tim McElwain. I had, however, given my word to Edinburgh and, after a couple of weeks of indecision, decided to honour that commitment and head for pastures new. Cathy was immensely helpful in accepting this decision.

She was, of course, fully aware of my discomfort at the Marsden, but her family and friends were all in the South, and whereas I would take my work with me, as it were, this was a big ask of her – and she was fully supportive.

When all the formalities were completed, I officially became the inaugural ICRF Professor of Medical Oncology in the University of Edinburgh on 1 April, 1979. The Marsden decided not to make any appointment to their chair, which remained vacant for the next twenty years.

In Edinburgh, medical oncology was to be based at the Western General Hospital alongside radiotherapy. To enable this, the top floor of the radiotherapy department had to be converted to provide clinical and office accommodation. Of course, that would take time. In consultation with the ICRF, the university suggested that I delay my arrival until the autumn of 1979, but they offered to put me on the payroll from April, and I was thus free to use the intervening six months in any appropriate way.

I had previously been introduced by Omar Yoder of EORTC to John Ultmann, the head of oncology at the University of Chicago, who invited me to join him for this period as associate director of medical research at the Billings Hospital in Hyde Park, South Chicago. We sold our home in Sutton, put everything in store and spent a memorable summer back in the USA, this time with our first daughter Sarah not yet two years old. Cathy did not take on paid work, but again she was supportive and enthusiastic, and we both enjoyed our time in Chicago. Given my new appointment in Edinburgh, it was particularly useful to be in a university clinical environment rather than an institutional one such as the NCI or the Marsden. In the latter institutions, patients are expected to enrol in research programmes so clinical activity can therefore be selective. In a university setting, all relevant clinical situations have to be catered for – routine as well as research.

One day in the early summer of 1979, I attended a Gordon Research Conference near Boston. These prestigious international conferences invite small numbers of experts to meet in plenary sessions for four to five days to focus on a specific medical or scientific theme. This particular conference was on the biochemistry of leukaemia, and I had been given a twenty-minute slot to present my work on ADA inhibitors as a new therapeutic target. My presentation was greeted with such interest that the organisers cancelled the rest of the morning's programme, and I held the floor in animated discussion for two whole hours. When I went into lunch, there were congratulations from many of the participants. I was on a high.

Then I was summoned to the phone. Cathy told me that my father had been referred to the Marsden, and I should phone my friend Michael Peckham, head of radiotherapy, to find out more. My father, he told me, had inoperable cancer of the oesophagus. I knew at once that that meant he only had a few months to live. Within a couple of hours, I had gone from the ego trip of a lifetime for my original research, to the knowledge that I was about to lose my father, with whom I had had such a complicated love/hate relationship. I left the conference, flew to London and took him for his first radiotherapy treatment, but had to return to Chicago soon afterwards.

He died three days before Christmas. When I returned to Chicago I wrote him a long letter, trying to assuage some of his understandable fear (he had suffered several frightening choking episodes) and repeating my explanation that his life expectancy depended in part on his response to treatment.

I also went back over our lives together, and thanked him for everything he had taught me when I was young and all that he had facilitated later. I pointed out that between us in just two generations we had come a long way from Sharpness to Edinburgh. I told him that I loved him.

In the event he did get some relief from the radiotherapy. With my mother he visited us once in Edinburgh around the time of my birthday in October, but his condition worsened soon after. We travelled south and I sat with him in hospital all through the night of 21 December. I held his hand and, although he drifted in and out of consciousness, he was peaceful. He died just after dawn the next day. When I went to the hospital to collect his possessions, I found my Chicago letter amongst them. My mother confirmed that it had meant a great deal to him, which was of some comfort to me. He is buried in the churchyard of a beautiful small church in the village of Tilford, near to their house in Farnham, Surrey. The church looks out over a small cricket green to the pub where we used to enjoy a pint on summer evenings. Later, when my mother and brother died, they were buried in the same place, which I visited recently. It has not changed in forty years – and hopefully never will.

The second half of 1979 had flown by at incredible speed. We left Chicago at the end of September and visited our families in England briefly en route for Edinburgh. There, we bought a ground-floor garden flat in the New Town – 9 Gloucester Place, not far from the Western General Hospital, where I was to be based.

Establishing Medical Oncology in Edinburgh

My first two to three years in Edinburgh were the busiest in my entire life. In the late 1970s, cancer was treated by surgeons and radiotherapists, although patients with leukaemias and lymphoma were referred to haematologists. I was keen to continue the development of my new drug deoxycoformycin, but as the relevant patients were already being cared for, it seemed inevitable that I could only take a minor share in the work of treating lymphomas and needed to create services for other cancers. I was, however, proud to be able to show the picture of a very young boy from Leith during my inaugural lecture. He had had a relapsed non-Hodgkin lymphoma and was the first patient to go into a complete remission as a result of treatment with DCF. The major development of the drug had to be left to others on both sides of the Atlantic, but I am proud of the fact that Pentostatin, as its trade name is known, is still listed in the British National Formulary. One other highlight of my DCF story, however, was an invitation to present it at a meeting of the New York Academy of Sciences in 1986. To get there, I had my first (of three) flights on Concorde. This was an extraordinary experience, unlike anything else that I have ever known on commercial flights. On the ground, passengers were treated like royalty, yet the plane's cabin was small, with only two seats on either side of the aisle. You were not allowed any significant hand-luggage, which particularly annoyed one of my fellow-passengers – the famous tennis player John McEnroe, who wanted to keep a special racket by his side. Food and champagne flowed, but the greatest thrill was the flying. During take-off you were really pressed back into your seat, like being in a fast speedboat. Flying at twice the speed of sound and at a height of 55,000 feet, looking out of the window you could actually see the curvature of the earth: we were almost in space! I was allowed into the cockpit to talk to the pilots, which was fun, and we arrived in New York less than three hours after we left London. Sadly, Concorde no longer flies but I was so fortunate to have had those three flight (two from London and one back from New York) in these magnificent aircraft. Those were the days …

My first impressions of medicine in Edinburgh were to recognise high standards of care – both in hospital and in general practice. In London, GPs showed little interest in medical oncology but they did in Edinburgh – and indeed they would query my clinical letters to them if they were not clear about prognosis, or what they should be looking out for in treated patients. As I expected, the hospital community wanted to test out whether this new, young, non-Edinburgh-trained professor was any good with patients. Oncology is a referred specialty, which means that patients would rarely be referred to me directly by GPs and this would mainly be from other physicians and surgeons who were usually responsible for making the diagnosis of cancer. From the very beginning, therefore, I received requests from a variety of consultants asking me to see their patients. It was tactful for me to visit them in the beds from which they were referred, and I therefore found myself visiting most of the hospitals in Edinburgh – the Royal Infirmary, of course, but also the Northern and Eastern General, the City, Longmore, Leith, the Deaconess, and – for me, the most challenging of all – the Royal Hospital for Sick Children. I was not trained in paediatric oncology but even at that time nearly all patients could be entered into national protocols. When necessary, I was able to seek advice from Professor Jim Malpas at Barts and Tim McElwain back at the Marsden, who were both experienced paediatric oncologists. All of this had to be initiated as a single-handed consultant, and I was therefore permanently on call, and usually working twelve-hour days. This put an enormous burden on Cathy, for whom the New Town of Edinburgh was an entirely unfamiliar environment. Fortunately, an old schoolfriend of hers lived nearby and was a source of friendship and very helpful advice, but with Sarah being just two years old, life for Cathy was hard. Nevertheless, she responded with typical courage and positivity. We were in this, after all, for the long game.

I was fortunate in my first year in Edinburgh to make two key appointments. The first was to find a secretary and, on advice of the executive dean, I appointed a truly wonderful person, Lyn Spencely. Lyn had previously been secretary to a recently retired professor of orthopaedics. She knew the NHS and the university very well and, apart from having excellent secretarial and personnel skills, was fluent in French and German. This really impressed my European colleagues, with whom I was trying to remain in contact during those first incredibly hectic years. By coincidence, Lyn's husband had been at Bryanston a few

The multidisciplinary team behind Edinburgh's first medical oncology unit at the Western General in 1981. Lyn Spencely is on my left and Jim Carmichael third in from the left. Our first lab technician, Sandra Laurie, is on the right.

years before me, and we all became friends. Her advice and counsel were of inestimable help to me, and when thirty years later, I spoke after dinner at my Festschrift, I was able to say with all honesty that medical oncology in Edinburgh would never have been the same without her.

The other key appointment was to recruit Jim Carmichael to be my first lecturer-registrar. Jim had trained in Edinburgh and therefore knew his way around and was an excellent young physician. He very quickly learnt the concepts that I was trying to introduce and was a tremendous support. Later on, after a research stint in our laboratories, I was able to help him obtain a fellowship at NCI, where he stayed for two years. A few years later he was appointed to be the first professor of medical oncology at Nottingham University.

In the 1980s the available anticancer drugs were only effective for a limited range of cancers. Furthermore, I clearly could not manage to see all the patients potentially referred to me, so I had to make some specific choices and explain these to all the colleagues who hoped for a clinical service. For reasons combining local needs with available useful therapies, I decided to concentrate on three areas: lung cancer, breast and ovarian cancer. In those days, the first of these was divided into two categories – small-cell and non-small cell lung cancer. Nowadays we recognise at least five subdivisions based on genetic knowledge. At that time, there was little that could be done to help non-small cell lung cancer, but the small-cell variant presented an interesting challenge. While most patients responded to initial chemotherapy, obtaining remissions that rapidly improved symptoms and prolonged useful life, almost all patients relapsed with resistance to further treatment, and died within two years. The challenge was to overcome this resistance.

I was fortunate that two excellent chest physicians at the Northern General Hospital, Ian Grant and Graham Crompton, were keen to enrol their patients into my clinical trials. We set up a joint clinic where every week we would see new patients together, and those meeting the relevant criteria were transferred to my ward at the Western.

My work at the Marsden and Brompton was well-known to the International Association for the Study of Lung Cancer and in 1981 I was invited to participate in its first workshop on small-cell lung cancer in the

For the team's 1985 Christmas party, I got out the old saxophone again.

magnificent setting of Ashford Castle on the west coast of Ireland. In 1984 I hosted my first international meeting in Edinburgh when I organised the association's second workshop at Gleneagles Hotel in Perthshire. The fifty-six participants came from nineteen countries in four continents, and during the four-day meeting I felt that Edinburgh had established a definite place in the international efforts to combat this particular cancer.

The university's professor of surgery, Sir Patrick Forrest, was keen to collaborate with us in medical oncology in studies of breast cancer and I helped to establish what became known as the Scottish Breast Cancer Trials, which made a significant contribution to the concept of adjuvant chemotherapy. This involved randomising woman who had had surgery to receive either four to six months of chemotherapy or a placebo. The results showed the benefit of post-operative chemotherapy, which became standard treatment thereafter. We were part of a large international effort to establish this concept, but we were the first in the world to take this idea further by exploring the value of chemotherapy *before* surgery for women with large or inoperable tumours. We published our results in *The Lancet* in the autumn of 1986 – the first publication of what is now widely adopted as 'neo-adjuvant' therapy for breast cancer.

My interest in ovarian cancer came from my time at the NCI, where Bob Young was a pioneer in the field. During my subsequent spell at the Royal Marsden, we had begun to explore the use of drugs based on the metal platinum. The first of these, cis-diaminedichloroplatinum (cisplatinum for short), had proved highly successful – indeed curative – for many patients in the treatment of testicular teratoma. It was also being trialled in cancer of the ovary. While clearly active, it was highly toxic: cisplatinum caused not only renal damage but was the most emetogenic drug we had ever encountered. The nausea and vomiting it caused was truly awful, and remedying this became an area of important research in Edinburgh. Work in the laboratories at the Marsden examined many analogues of cisplatinum, resulting in the development of the much less toxic drug carboplatin, which is widely used today.

Soon after arriving in Edinburgh, I was introduced to two gynaecologists who were responsible for the management of ovarian cancer. Dr George Smart and Dr Jeremy Livingstone invited me to join their weekly meeting with referring colleagues, radiation oncologists and pathologists in what were the first truly multidisciplinary meetings of their kind. Now commonplace, this was unusual in the early 1980s and provided a perfect opportunity for me to introduce everyone to what we could or could not expect from medical oncology.

Apart from setting up clinical trials for women with this particularly unpleasant condition, I was keen to establish laboratory research with human samples of ovarian cancer. The latter grows freely in the peritoneal (abdominal) fluid called ascites, which can be easily obtained from patients. Others had shown that this situation could be mimicked in the laboratory by growing human ovarian cancer cells in tissue culture. Most samples, however, only survived for a few days or weeks, but occasionally a cell line could be established, giving durable cells that allowed full experimentation.

When I arrived in Edinburgh, there was no laboratory space available. I had made it clear at my interview that while I hoped that we would be able to collaborate with established scientists in the city, I would seek to establish my own laboratory primarily to carry out pharmacological studies and drug development using human tumours, not the more usual animal ones.

The ICRF endowment to establish the chair of medical oncology, matched by the NHS Lothian Health Board, generously provided for clinical and administrative staff. However, to fund laboratory research I had to make new applications and, in discussion with the senior ICRF staff, it was agreed that the fund would establish an extramural unit in Edinburgh, a similar arrangement to the ones that existed at St Bartholomew's and Guy's hospitals in London. I was appointed director of this unit and I recognised my good fortune in that, once I had outlined my initial research proposals, ICRF agreed to award five years' worth of funding to create a laboratory with an initial staff of six. The programme would be subject to quinquennial review, and I subsequently survived four of these very thorough assessments. It was a huge bonus that I did not have to spend my first years in Edinburgh writing grants in the usual way. There was so much else to do.

Having persuaded the administration at the Western General Hospital to allow me to occupy a vacant site at the front of the campus, with help from experts in ICRF we bought a prefabricated laboratory, equipped it and advertised for staff. My first appointment was to be my senior laboratory technician for the next twenty-five years. Sandra Lawrie was not only a very competent laboratory worker, but over the years developed excellent skills in personnel management, administration and finance. She had 'green fingers' for tissue culture work, and it was due to these skills that we had our first successful result. Sandra worked on many samples of ovarian cancer, all fresh from patients. Eventually, she developed a cell line – a strain of identical cells that keep self-reproducing – that we called PE01. The latter came from a woman with advanced ovarian cancer who was treated with cisplatin and went into complete remission. When she subsequently relapsed, we were able to harvest some of her malignant cells and create a second cell line, PE04. The patient was treated again and proved to be cisplatin-resistant. We published the characterization of these two cell lines in the *International Journal of Cancer* in 1987. Cytologically, they were indistinguishable as ovarian cancer cells, but they showed significant chromosomal changes and, of course, differing sensitivity to cisplatin. Derived from the same patient at different times, this represented a unique model, and there were many requests from laboratories all over the world to obtain samples. The cell lines were subsequently managed by ICRF centrally to keep a record both of their use and the research published as a result.

Amid all this frenetic work, family life continued. On 2 December 1980, our second daughter, Anna, was born at the Western General. We were both thrilled, and she has been a source of immense pride and joy to Cathy and me ever since. However, when Anna was only ten months old when, while on our summer holiday in 1981, I received a call from the Royal Marsden to explain that my mother had been diagnosed with inoperable lung cancer. It was less than two years since my father's death, and she had never really got over his loss. Cancer often develops in bereaved people, and this was a classic example. As was the case with my father's illness, it was frustratingly difficult to take time off to go from Edinburgh to the Brompton Hospital in London for unsatisfactorily short visits, but she was well looked after – for radiotherapy by my former partner Jo Ford whom I had worked with when I was treating lung cancer at the Marsden, and for her terminal care at the Brompton Hospital's county branch in Frimley, by a consultant who had been a fellow student from my medical school days. During my last visit, we both knew exactly what was happening, but I was not there when a short time later she died on 19 October. She was only sixty-seven. We buried her with my father at Tilford.

Yet the worst tragedy was still to come. After my

mother's death, my brother Robert and I inherited a relatively small amount of money. For me, this equated to about a year's salary – very useful but not life-changing. However, for Robert this was a very significant amount. After leaving the Royal Academy of Music in London he had never established a proper career. He did some teaching and earned some money playing in clubs and bars (he was as talented at light music as at classical), but he had not inherited our father's work ethic as I had. His brief marriage to a lovely Barts nurse broke down after the birth of their son, who sadly had a rare condition called Noonan's Syndrome, which is associated with complex mental and physical problems. For a couple of summers, Robert got work as an entertainer on cruise liners sailing out of Piraeus in Greece, and that is where he decided to go once we had sorted out our mother's estate. Our earlier closeness had gone and we had drifted apart, and throughout 1982 I only heard from him twice, by short letters with no return address. Shortly before Christmas, I received a letter telling me that he had run out of money, felt a complete failure, and intended to end his life. I had no address, and had no way to find him. In spite of the impulse to do so, I realised that there was no point in going to Athens and hoped that this was just a passing *cri de coeur*, but just after Christmas a second letter arrived, confirming his intentions. A few days later a policewoman arrived at our front door to say that Robert's body had been found in his car, with death due to carbon monoxide poisoning. Suicide is truly awful. Sadly, it is not rare, and I have several close friends who have lost siblings this way, and for any family the sense of loss is heightened by the inevitable feeling that one should have been able to do more to prevent such tragic loss of life.

I decided to have Robert's body returned for cremation in England. This involved me having to go to a mortuary in London to identify his body. As a doctor, I knew exactly what is involved in having a post-mortem and Robert had had two – one in Greece and the other in London, since at that time smugglers were using bodies to transport drugs. He was barely recognisable, and it took me some time to get over this ghastly event. At his funeral service I read a passage from TS Eliot's *The Wasteland*, and his ashes were interred with our parents in Tilford churchyard. In my first three years in Edinburgh, I had only seen my extended family three times, on each occasion for a funeral.

These reflections are not the place to detail all the developments of the next thirty years of medical oncology in Edinburgh, but I will mention just a few of the highlights.

With the rapid development of the specialty in other universities in the UK there arose tensions within the medical profession, most particularly between medical oncologists, radiotherapists and haematologists concerning patient 'ownership' – a less than attractive attribute of the various medical fiefdoms. In Edinburgh, I had decided to leave the haematological malignancies in the hands of haematologists and was fortunate that there was very little private practice in the oncology setting – a major source of interprofessional rivalry elsewhere. My clinical facilities were shared with the radiotherapists, and it made sense to join forces with the head of radiotherapy, Professor William Duncan, to create a single department of clinical oncology. We got agreement from both the NHS and the university to achieve this, and Bill Duncan became head of the NHS side and I the head of the university department. We alternated this on a three-yearly basis. Our aim was not just to maximise the use of all our physical resources, but to teach and train young doctors in the important aspects of both disciplines. Thus, my trainee fellows would spend time in radiation oncology (as it became known), and I would routinely have radiation trainees on my ward rounds and clinics. Later on, this model was adopted by many other medical schools, but at the time it was unique – another first for Edinburgh.

Despite the academic rewards of our research and the welcome provided by my local colleagues, many of our clinical outcomes remained poor, and many of our patients died from their cancers. The discipline that we now recognise as palliative care did not exist as such in the 1980s, but in Edinburgh, under the inspired guidance of Dr Derek Doyle, they had established St Columba's Hospice – only the second of its kind in the UK, after the example of Dame Cicely Saunders's St Christopher's in London. Derek was an inspirational physician and teacher, and far from being suspicious of our use of chemotherapy – as so many were – he welcomed me and my trainees. We developed an excellent partnership between the hospital and the hospice. I served for many years on the board of governors at Saint Columba's and some years later persuaded them to release £1 million to establish a chair of palliative medicine in the university. The appointee, Professor Marie Fallon, is one of the finest doctors with whom I have worked, and she continues the theme of excellence associated with Derek Doyle, but now adding a major research programme which is internationally recognised. On reflection, this was one of the most rewarding achievements of all my years in Edinburgh.

Research into the problem of emesis – the nausea and vomiting associated with many anticancer treatments – was another success. In the mid-1980s, we recognised our weakness in managing this problem and asked whether we could apply the principles of clinical pharmacology to the use of the available anti-emetics. We experimented with varying doses and combinations of these drugs and published some marginally interesting results in the literature. To my great good fortune, these were picked up by a group of scientists working under the leadership of Dr Mike Tyers at Glaxo in London.

In the summer of 1986, he visited me in Edinburgh. He explained his recent work on emesis and the discovery of an inhibitor of the 5 hydroxy-tryptamine receptor (5HT3), a proposed key trigger for emesis in response to some anti-cancer drugs. Having done some dose-finding experiments with volunteers, he asked if we would be willing to conduct a clinical and pharmacological evaluation on our patients receiving platinum chemotherapy. I was intrigued and we quickly obtained all the necessary permissions for a trial. As a result, I wrote what I believe to be the first prescription ever for Ondansetron – the drug in question – for a patient with cancer. We treated three young men with testicular cancer and two of them experienced no sickness at all. It worked! Exploration of this drug and Granisetron – a similar one owned by Smith Kline Beecham in the

US – moved very rapidly, and I soon became part of a small group of international 'eccentrics' (as some of our friends referred to us for focusing on emesis), but we had found something of inestimable value to patients with so many different cancers. With funding from several pharmaceutical companies, we met twice a year for several years – in the winter at Mottaret in the French Alps, and in the summer at Quinto de Lago in Portugal – to share our experience and refine our protocols. Yes, we really worked hard in these wonderful places, but the skiing and golf were rewarding too! Of all the research that I have ever undertaken, I believe that this development of 5HT3 antiemetics was the most useful. Their use is now routine worldwide.

Some years after this I was again approached by Glaxo to ask if I would be prepared to help them with a legal case. The generic company Teva had started marketing their version of Ondansetron eighteen months before it came off Glaxo's patent. I had done a certain amount of legal work in the UK regarding patent mismanagement, but never anything of the order of this huge commercial challenge. Over the course of the next year, I flew to New York on several occasions to brief a very impressive lawyer in his Park Avenue office about the early development of Ondansetron. The case all revolved around what was, or was not, known around the time of my first use of the drug in 1986. Having been so directly involved, I was very clear that Mike Tyers' invention was original. When the case came to court, I was Glaxo's star witness. I was well prepared by their lawyer for the interrogation I could expect from the opposition. The first approach would be to try to trash my credentials. Sure enough, soon after being sworn in and having acknowledged that I was a 'full' professor of medicine in the University of Edinburgh, I was asked 'is Edinburgh a regular university?' Sitting proudly upright (I was seated on a sort of throne immediately to the left of the judge) I answered in a confident voice 'Yes sir, actually Edinburgh has been a regular university for over 400 years!' The judge stifled a laugh, the barrister looked very crestfallen – and three days later we won the case.

Throughout my time as director of the ICRF unit in Edinburgh, I was invited to sit on national cancer research committees within the ICRF, the Cancer Research Campaign, the Medical Research Council and the UK Coordinating Committee for Cancer Research, for which I chaired their lung cancer sub-committee. While adding considerably to my already heavy workload in Edinburgh, this experience helped me greatly in learning how to write our own grants. The greatest challenge in this regard was preparing for the ICRF quinquennial reviews, which I led on four occasions. I remember them all very well.

ICRF Quinquennial Reviews

These were formal, detailed examinations of a group or unit's achievements and proposals for the next five-year period. I have kept copies of my four quinquennial submissions and they cast an interesting light on the extraordinary changes and progress that occurred over two decades.

1986: The papers we submitted for this first review were almost all written by me, explaining how I had gone about establishing the extramural unit within the university's department of clinical oncology and built up a team of young enthusiastic researchers. We were a small group of sixteen people – clinical, nursing, data management and laboratory staff – but between us I reported sixty-three published papers, contributions to eleven books and seventy presentations at national or international meetings.

The review took place over two days and was conducted by a team of four external assessors, two members of ICRF council and their director, Sir Walter Bodmer. I was fortunate in the selection of the externals – George Canellos, a senior medical oncologist from Harvard, and one of the founding fathers of medical oncology in the USA; Derek Crowther, the professor of medical oncology from Manchester, who had been on my appointment committee for the chair in Edinburgh; Bob Pinedo, a friend from NCI days, then head of medical oncology at the Free University Hospital in Amsterdam; and Professor Mel Stevens from Aston University, an expert on experimental drug development.

After only six years in Edinburgh, I was confident about our clinical programme. We had settled in well with colleagues throughout the city, were already recognised for our high standard of patient care and had created an excellent platform for clinical research. The review committee acknowledged this and were generous in their praise in the subsequent written review from their visit. Both they and I were more concerned about our laboratory programme. Clearly, we needed a senior scientist to lead the young team I had assembled in the lab, but it was proving difficult to find the right person.

The term translational research' was not in use in those days, but I was determined that our laboratory should focus on human tumours, not the animal ones used by so many other laboratories. We had already developed the ovarian cancer cell lines PE01 and PE04 and were studying human tumour biopsies in xenograft systems to mimic the clinical situation as closely as possible. Scientists love clean, safe reproducible models, and clinical material provides anything but this. I have enjoyed teasing Sir Walter Bodmer's successor Sir Paul Nurse that to win his Nobel Prize he stuck to the simple yeast – not even mice! To find a world-class scientist willing to work in the highly complex and heterogeneous world of human tumours proved a major problem throughout all my years as director in Edinburgh. It is interesting, if frustrating to read in the 1986 review summary from the ICRF, that 'a very suitable applicant had recently declined the appointment for domestic reasons'. That person subsequently became an FRS and President of the Institute of Cancer Research in London. We could probably have made him famous even earlier, but such is life, and he remains a good friend to this day.

1991: By now, the unit was ten years old, and we had increased the ICRF staff to forty-nine people. We recorded in the previous five years two hundred and fifty-two papers, thirty-four book contributions and two hundred and fifty-three presentations at national and international meetings. Our clinical programme had continued to develop well and we were recognised as one of the major oncology research centres in Europe. At the time of the review, I was also about

At Edinburgh University's medical graduations with the Dean, Professor Christopher Edwards, in 1995, when I was faculty promoter.

to take over as President of the European Society of Medical Oncology (ESMO).

Our laboratory programme had progressed well under the direction of Bill Miller, an expert on breast cancer biology. We had established a productive collaboration with the MRC's Human Genetics Unit to study the molecular genetics of familial and sporadic ovarian cancer. To accommodate the appointment of three tenured scientists, we had undergone major refurbishment of our laboratories, which now occupied the top floor of the MRC building on the Western General Hospital campus.

The most exciting new development that we reported at this time was of a programme of psychosocial oncology headed by Dr Ann Cull. Ann was a highly respected clinical psychologist at the Western General who had at first been involved with the unit on a part-time basis but from 1989 was on an ICRF-supported secondment. She established a programme examining the psychological outcome of treatment for patients with gynaecological malignancies that aimed to identify cognitive, affective and behavioural components of their experience which might be amenable to change. A second initiative on neuropsychological assessment focused on the neurotoxicity of interferons that were being widely trialled at that time, the late effects of radiation to the brain, and the neuropsychological outcomes for adults with brain tumours. A third major initiative was to explore how to predict the patients at risk of serious psychological morbidity from routine treatments, and to evaluate intervention strategies. Ann's programme was very highly rated by the review committee, and she was awarded tenure by ICRF to focus full-time on this innovative work.

1996: This was probably the most successful of all that I oversaw. Paul Nurse had replaced Walter Bodmer as director of the ICRF and in addition to four other directors, he bought seven external experts to review our work. During the previous five years, there had been major changes in the NHS with the formation of independent trusts. In Edinburgh this resulted in significant differences between our two main teaching hospitals – the Royal Infirmary and the Western General – which had a detrimental effect on clinical trials, and research in general. Fortunately, I was asked to serve as the university's non-executive director on the Western General Trust Board. The medical school was one of only three in the UK to have been given the highest rating by a UK-wide Research Assessment Exercise and I was able to keep the importance of research on the trust's agenda. The government had recently published their report, A Policy Framework for Commissioning Cancer Services, by Sir Kenneth Calman, and I was invited to chair a working party on behalf of the Royal College of Physicians and Surgeons in Scotland to discuss the consequences of the Calman reforms. To date most of the medical oncology consultants in the UK had been funded through university contracts, and there was agreement on the need to increase the number of oncologists paid for by the NHS. This would allow ICRF, CRC and other charity and university-funded staff more time for research.

Another major change in clinical practice around this

time was that oncologists were beginning to specialise in just one or two diseases. Thus, we saw the development of multidisciplinary groups for breast, lung, colorectal cancer etc, to which each would have specialist medical oncology input. I took responsibility for patients with gynaecological cancers and melanomas. In those days, we had very few active treatments for patients with melanoma, but that facilitated ethical participation in experimental therapy as first-line treatment. Both of these clinical areas fitted well with our laboratory research.

After an intensive review from this large and impressive committee, we were awarded the ICRF rating of 'work which is at the forefront internationally and which it is judged will have an important and substantial impact'. I was particularly pleased with two of the written comments, one about my drug development programme, and the other about Ann's psychosocial programme. Of the former they wrote 'this is an excellent unit with identifiable strengths, in particular the links between clinical practice and the laboratory exemplified by the drug development programme'. This was exactly what I had set out to achieve from the very beginning. Of Ann's programme they commented that she 'is an exceptionally gifted and productive academic. This original programme seeks to address several unique, yet interconnected issues faced by cancer patients'. They recognised her international reputation as she was about to become chairman of the EORTC quality of life group and unanimously agreed to give her tenure. Everyone concerned was delighted with this outcome, but I was especially thrilled. Apart from enjoying her academic success as a colleague, I had the year before this asked her to be my wife and she had said 'yes'!

2001: This took place in December at a time of major administrative change, both in the university and the NHS, while the ICRF were in the process of discussing a merger with the other major cancer research organisation in the UK, the Cancer Research Campaign. This became a reality just over a year after this review. Our drug development programme continued apace, now increasingly led by Duncan Jodrell, who was later recruited to a chair of cancer therapeutics at Cambridge University. The cancer genetics programme led by Hani Gabra received particularly strong support, so it was no surprise when, three years later, he was headhunted to a chair at Imperial College, London. Ann's psychosocial oncology again received high marks and her future proposals focused on methods to improve our ability to collect and analyse quality of life data, and the problem of understanding fatigue. The latter has become an area of great importance with the development of immunotherapy, and it is rewarding that the issue of understanding patients' experience (quality of life issues) is now taken very seriously by the regulators of new drug licences – the European Medicines Agency and, in the US, the Food and Drug Administration.

Around the time of the 2001 review Ann became aware of an unprecedented opportunity to develop her specialty throughout the NHS in Scotland. The government created a new position to spearhead this through the Scottish Council for Postgraduate Education, and Ann was headhunted – initially on a part-time basis – to help us with the forthcoming site-visit but then full-time. Unsurprisingly, she proved a great success, and in recognition of overcoming some particular hurdles in the West of Scotland, Glasgow University awarded her an honorary chair. Now there were two Professors Smyth.

Following our successful review in 1996, I had held several lengthy discussions with Paul Nurse about the continuing problem of attracting world-class laboratory scientists. It was clear to me that with the expansion of the existing programme, we simply did not have enough free space to attract candidates of that calibre. With Paul's encouragement and the eventual approval of the university and NHS (not easily obtained), I set about planning and funding an entire new building to house our multidisciplinary team, but mostly to provide new state-of-the-art laboratories. Academics are not renowned for their skills in building design, or accurate financial planning, and I had experienced a near-disaster on the Western General's campus a few years before. The Molecular Medicine Centre was created by four separate academic departments, all with different opinions about lab layout, seminar space, social space and the like. The result was far from satisfactory, and it was even joked that the fact that the lifts reached all floors was a surprise. With this and other experiences in mind, I resolved to take as much advice as possible from my team, but then to design the building with expert architects essentially to my specification alone. The appointed architects could not believe their luck, dealing with only one academic, not teams of them, as had been their previous experience.

By the time of the 2001 review, I had raised the £7 million required and planned a 2,000 sq m building over four floors immediately next to our old accommodation in the MRC building. At the time of the review the superstructure of the building was complete, but we only moved into the complete facility in 2002. The top two floors were wet labs and the other two offices, seminar and meeting rooms, as well as an audio-visual studio, a social space, and stores. I was thrilled with the outcome, and we had a very memorable celebration in December of that year when the building was officially opened by HRH the Princess Royal, who is now the chancellor of Edinburgh University.

Buildings are, of course, nothing like as important as people, and in earlier days I had carried out some of my most important research in old, totally unsuitable accommodation. However, by the time I retired from my chair and left the Western General, I felt very proud of leaving this lasting visible statement of all the progress that collectively we had achieved. Even now I still feel a little glow of pride when I pass this building.

My Contribution to European Oncology

For over forty years I have taken a major part in the development of medical oncology in Europe, and I am still actively involved. After my experience at the NCI and with encouragement from the then director Vince De Vita, I became involved with the European Organisation for the Research and Treatment of Cancer. Its pharmacokinetics and metabolism group flourished, and I enjoyed hosting a joint meeting between them and the early clinical trials group in Edinburgh. I was subsequently invited to join the organisation's board, and served on it for many years. Between 2001-10 I was

With Professor Colin Bird at the topping out ceremony for our new research building at the Western General in 2001.

The finished building 2001.

editor-in-chief of their journal, *The European Journal of Cancer*, which was hard work but an amazing source of continued professional education. During the 1990s, the European Society for Medical Oncology (ESMO) played a major role in establishing training programmes for this new specialty throughout Europe. I served as their president from 1991-3. With strong support from the surgical and radiation oncology community, we formed the Federation of European Cancer Societies to foster interdisciplinary research and thinking. I served as its president between 2005-7 but to my great dismay ESMO – my own specialty group – decided to withdraw from the federation and hold their own separate meetings and activities. This was a backward step, and hugely disruptive to the political activities the federation had engaged in with the European Commission. Privately, I was furious, but I did what I could to keep the ideas behind the federation active. Changes were inevitable, part of which was recognised when I changed its name to the European Cancer Organisation. We almost collapsed but the meeting over which I presided in Barcelona in 2007 still had 16,000 participants.

Throughout my years of involvement in European oncology we have witnessed the transition in drug development from academic institutions to the pharmaceutical industry. In the 1980s the pharmaceutical industry came on board with their much greater resources and partnered the best science from academia not only to identify new potential drugs, but to speed up the process – all the way from initial patent of a new idea to the new drug's availability for patients. Both from the clinicians' and the industrial perspective, we were all concerned to speed up the careful analysis of new drugs while in clinical trial, and to make them as widely available as possible once they were licensed. Despite enormous progress, this remains a huge problem. Patent life is only twenty years and if too much of that time is used up in research and development, including assessment by regulators, then the costs become unacceptably high. Under patent, only the licence holder can market the drug, but once the patent has expired any (generic) company can make and sell the same drug. Inevitably, generic drugs are much cheaper because the manufacturer has not incurred all the research costs. For new anticancer medicines, the total cost of developing a new effective drug from the initial idea stage, through all the preclinical laboratory work, toxicology and the various stages of clinical trial is currently quoted at around \$1.5 billion. If only ten or twelve years of patent protection is left, companies launch their new drug at a very high price.

Working closely with the Medical and Healthcare products Regulatory Authority (MHRA) in the UK, new medicines are assessed for safety, efficacy and quality by the Commission on Human Medicines (CHM). Its predecessor was the Committee on Safety of Medicines (CSM), whose chairman, Sir Alasdair Breckenridge, asked me to join as their first expert on oncology drugs. I served on the committee for the next six years until it transformed to become the CHM. By this time there were so many new anticancer drug applications that we formed a specialist subcommittee for oncology and haematology, which I chaired from 2006 to 2013. In this capacity I continued to attend the commission's meetings and I also served on the European Medicines Agency's first scientific advisory group for oncology.

This experience with the licensing authorities was both interesting and an excellent form of continuing professional education – particularly important for professors and directors of cancer centres. My combined experience with the science of drug development and knowledge of challenges facing regulators has led to invitations to serve on advisory boards for a number of pharmaceutical companies, an activity that I still pursue. This is completely *bona fide* on the clear understanding that any conflict of interest will be declared to the regulators if there is any personal involvement with any particular product or company under assessment.

Since retiring from the chair of medical oncology in Edinburgh, I have helped to form the Cancer Drug Development Forum, whose board I currently chair. This is a not-for-profit association based in Brussels, bringing together in workshops researchers, people from the industry, regulators, health technology assessors and representatives of patient advisory groups in order to understand the challenges of drug development from all its constituent parts. We are making real progress in reducing the time taken from new idea to available medicine, with fewer patients needed for pivotal trials, but we have yet to make progress in reducing the high costs of new drugs.

9. FAMILY LIFE

Nothing matters more to me than my family. In most aspects of this I have been very lucky, but there are two exceptions: my brother's suicide and the fact that my first marriage ended in divorce. As a young man I had found commitment to marriage difficult, but for most of the sixteen years Cathy and I were married, we were happy. She was incredibly supportive of the work choices that I made, which posed several upheavals for her, and also of all the travel I undertook, leaving her alone with our children, Sarah and Anna. Unquestionably, our greatest achievement was to produce two such wonderful daughters. They are both intelligent, industrious, musical people and popular amongst their many friends. They both enjoyed their schooldays at Mary Erskine School in Edinburgh, before going to university – Sarah to Cambridge and Anna to Newcastle.

In their childhood I particularly enjoyed our summer holidays – especially the camping trips to France. One of the most adventurous of these was when we towed a caravan, with a small dinghy on top of the car, all the way to the Dordogne. By mistake we arrived at Paris's Periphérique (ring road) just in time for the rush hour on a Friday afternoon – a driver's worst nightmare. The girls loved the cross-Channel ferries (our family's WhatsApp is called Crispy Sheets after Sarah's passion for the Brittany Ferries bed linen in the overnight cabins), camping and the open air and the warm sea and sunshine – sadly a rare event in Scottish summers.

The one great sadness for them and for me was when Cathy decided to end our marriage. In 1988-9 I was aware that we were becoming more distant from each other. I was working far too hard and travelling a lot.

I was very aware of not pulling my weight – as husband and father – at that time as work was all- consuming. To address this imbalance in my life, I obtained permission from the university to take a year's sabbatical, from the autumn of 1989, mostly to regain closeness with Cathy. But our marriage was over.

I was keen to retain our home in Inverleith and so Cathy rented a flat nearby to make it easier for the children to move between the two of us. The next few months were the worst I have ever experienced. One of the awful things about divorce is that, for the first time in my life, I was not in control of my own destiny. Lawyers, mortgage lenders, bankers, and pension advisers were all telling me what I could and could not do. The law requires that a couple divide all their assets 50:50 and is not interested in apportioning blame or reasons for a divorce.

The year immediately after Cathy left was very difficult for me. Having been granted sabbatical leave, I was of course not able to use it as I had envisaged, as most of it was needed for sorting out my financial affairs. I was hard up and lonely, but when I did return to work, my colleagues were very kind and understanding. Others covered for me in committees and travel. Cathy and I shared time with the girls, who spent two nights a week and alternate weekends with me. On the relevant days I would leave clinics early to collect them from school and, contrary to my previous life, would take time off work to attend school concerts and sporting and other events with them.

Both girls were immensely brave. Sadly, because divorce is all too common, they knew friends in similar situations. I think that in many ways school gave them security in an otherwise confusing world. We had great holidays together – just the three of us. Weekends on Loch Tay (where I kept a small boat), camping trips to France, and visits to my family in the West Country are all happy memories of that time.

I survived and, after a while, my good fortune returned. Her name is Ann! Among the girls' friends were Ann's two daughters, Gillian and Laura, and the four of them enjoyed sleepovers at each other's houses at weekends. Ann was a colleague of mine at work, but with the increasing friendship of our four girls we found ourselves spending more and more time in each other's company. Ann's divorce from a neurologist at the Western General Hospital was resolved in a much more amicable fashion than mine. Having fallen in love, we decided to get married.

Our wedding in St Giles' Cathedral on 6 May, 1995, fully restored my faith in humanity. It was a really wonderful celebration of love and friendship, with so many family and friends travelling from far and wide to be with us. The organist at St Giles, Herrick Bunney, played magnificently, the choir's singing was glorious,

Our wedding day, 6 May 1995

and all four girls participated. Anna and Gillian each read a lesson, Laura sang, and Sarah played the violin in a quartet of her friends. Deservedly, they were all loudly applauded at the reception we held afterwards in the Royal College of Physicians. We honeymooned in Barbados and life was off to a new start.

In 2020 we marked our twenty-fifth wedding anniversary – sadly not celebrated because of the Covid pandemic, but I enjoyed looking back on that quarter-century all the same. Second marriages are very different to first ones, and of course there have been some bumpy moments along the way. Overall, though, I believe that we have made a success of it. I love Ann very much and feel loved by her and all four of our daughters. Our love for them was one of the major things that brought us together in the first place and seeing them now – all in their early forties, all married with successful careers and marriages of their own – is a source of enormous pleasure and pride for us both.

I do not think it is appropriate to write at length about our girls for fear of intruding on their privacy, but I admire how much effort they have all put into keeping in touch with each other as their lives have diverged, and developing close relationships with us as stepfather and stepmother. They have each made a huge contribution to their new life in this extended family. We have a large collection of photo albums of wonderful Christmases at home in Inverleith. Everyone has contributed to other important family occasions – graduations, weddings, christenings and special birthdays. For my seventieth birthday, we rented a large house in Perthshire and all of them came with husbands and children for a wonderful few days. For Ann's seventieth we repeated the experience, this time at a manor house in Gloucestershire, where, to the obvious anxiety of all our grandchildren, Ann distinguished herself by doing a 'wing walk' strapped to the upper wing of a Boeing Stearman, sadly not piloted by me but by an expert display pilot.

We now have ten grandchildren – each of the girls has two children, except Sarah who has four. Five boys and five girls and they are all delightful. This is a grandparental view – parents would probably add 'most of the time'. Sadly, the Covid pandemic limited the time that we can spend with them, especially Gillian's family who were then living in New York. We communicate as best we can by phone and social media. All through the pandemic, I longed for the time when we could give them all a hug again.

To celebrate her seventieth birthday Ann did a 'Wing Walk' on this Boeing Stearman watched by our four girls – Anna, Gillian, Sarah and Laura.

*My father with his first granddaughter, Sarah, in 1977,
and me with mine, Sarah's Lucy in 2004.*

10. MEETING THE
ROYAL FAMILY

Over the years, I have met a number of members of the Royal Family, whom I hold in the highest regard. Their ability to conduct themselves with grace while meeting countless strangers for the briefest of conversations, yet to convey such an apparent interest in all concerned, is truly remarkable.

I first met the Queen in London when she visited the ICRF headquarters in Lincoln's Inn Fields in London, in the early 1980s. She had not known that its work now extended to Edinburgh and showed genuine interest on learning about what we were creating there.

In 2002 I met the Royal Family three times. In March, I was invited to a reception at Buckingham Palace to mark the launch of Cancer Research UK. My colleague from Edinburgh, Sir David Carter, more used to such events than I, suggested that we position ourselves near a particular entrance from which the drinks were served. The Royals are famous for their liquid hospitality, and the gin and tonic from the offered tray was like a strong dry martini. Not having eaten all day, I took the second one very slowly. In May I was one of a large gathering of guests for a similar reception at the Palace of Holyroodhouse, and in December the Princess Royal officially opened our new Cancer Research building, of which more later.

I met the Queen on two occasions at the Western General. The first was when she opened our new day-care facilities in the oncology department, and the second when she officially opened the Wellcome Trust Clinical Research Centre, of whose scientific advisory committee I was chair. On the latter occasion, I introduced her to a group of women of her own age who had taken part in what became known as the Lothian Birth Cohort Studies. In 1999 Edinburgh University's Professor of Differential Psychology, Ian Deary, formed this to revisit two mental health surveys carried out on eleven-year-old schoolchildren in 1932 and 1947. He contacted as many survivors of these studies as possible, now in their seventies, and retested them with the same questionnaires as originally used. This was to investigate how childhood intelligence relates to cognitive ability, and mental, physical and brain health in older age. The Queen was fascinated and of course the women were thrilled by her conversation.

My most private meeting with the Queen and the Duke of Edinburgh took place in Paris in April 2004. They were on a state visit to France to celebrate the centenary of the Entente Cordiale between our two countries. On 6 April six cancer researchers – three each from the UK and France – were invited to spend the day in conference to explore ways of increasing collaboration. I was one of the UK delegates, but unfortunately – and unusually – my health let me down. The night before, while attending a concert in the Queen's Hall in Edinburgh, I suffered

Being greeted by the Queen for a dinner at the British Embassy in Paris, 2004.

*With Princess Anne and Edinburgh University Principal Sir Timothy O'Shea
at the official opening of the new Cancer Research building in 2002.*

a severe attack of abdominal pain. Much against my wife's wishes, I took the dawn flight to Paris and, pain-free, managed to join the academic discussions. The real treat of this event was to be invited to a private dinner with the Queen and Duke at the British Embassy that night. On arrival in Paris, I realised that I was becoming jaundiced – at that time of undiagnosed cause but, being an oncologist, I feared the worst. At the sumptuous dinner, I hardly ate anything and decided that alcohol was a definite no-no. I still have the menu, and I missed out on a Pol Roger Cuvée Sir Winston Churchill (1995) and a 1985 Château Margaux. Two days later, I had my gall bladder removed at the Edinburgh Royal Infirmary, relieved that the diagnosis of cholecystitis was not what I had feared.

The Duke of Edinburgh was for many years chancellor of Edinburgh University and on several occasions it was my turn to look after him at less formal meetings. He was well-known for his wicked sense of humour and was very direct in his conversation but had a remarkable capacity for putting strangers at ease.

Princess Anne has succeeded her father as chancellor and spends a considerable amount of time at the university. Like her father, she has the knack of effortlessly engaging strangers in normal conversation. My best encounter with her was in December 2002, when she came to officially open the new cancer research building at the Western General. After all the formal introductions, I spent half an hour showing her around, introducing her to members of staff and explaining our philosophy of multidisciplinary working. The building was intended as the central hub for all the various activities of the whole cancer centre. She toured the laboratories, where we had laid on some demonstrations, and was particularly interested to hear something of our psychosocial work and innovations in palliative care research. We gathered senior members of the university and the Western General Trust in our brand-new seminar room, and there were the usual speeches and an unveiling of a commemorative plaque. It was a memorable day and I was very touched by the 'Thank you' letter that I received shortly after.

Of all the members of the Royal Family I have met, I have most enjoyed the times with Prince Charles. He inherited his father's sense of humour and we have had some great laughs together. I particularly remember when he was to visit the oncology department at the Western General to review some major refurbishments. As the visit was to be on a Friday, my clinic day, I was asked to present at least one patient to him. This request came some three or four months prior to the visit and, for security reasons, I was asked to identify the patient whom I would present. Four months in oncology is a long time, so it was not an easy task to identify someone who was likely to be well and interesting for Prince Charles so far in advance. Fortune was with me when I chose Mr B – a retired boatman from Leith who, some years earlier, had had a thumb amputated for malignant melanoma. A missing digit allowed me to present the case without the need for any undressing, and the story was interesting because Mr B had subsequently developed metastases in his liver. To everyone's delight, he had responded unusually well to a research drug and was now well. So it was a good story to tell. I explained to Mr B that when Prince Charles arrived, he would probably be accompanied into my consulting room by a security person, but to our mutual delight, on arrival Prince Charles closed the door and the three of us were alone. After I presented the case, Prince Charles engaged Mr B in typically friendly conversation, and from being a very nervous wreck, Mr B relaxed. To my horror Prince Charles then undid a cufflink, rolled up his sleeve and asked my opinion about a swelling on his forearm. Totally unprepared, I reached for my specs and, having absolutely no idea what this was (but confident that it was not a melanoma) I advised him that it would probably be best to have it surgically excised for pathological examination. 'Interesting, professor,' said Prince Charles. 'That is not what my doctors in London have recommended.' Mr B leaned forward, prodding Prince Charles on his shoulder. 'If I was you, I would listen to the professor,' he said. Prince Charles and I both burst into laughter. A stunned Mr B suddenly realised that he could be accused of assaulting the heir to the throne – but nonetheless the event concluded in good spirits.

I have also met Prince Charles through his patronage of the Monteverdi Choir. He is a personal friend of Sir John Eliot Gardiner, with whom he shares a passion for organic farming: when they are together, they inevitably talk about breeding cattle. Prince Charles has been immensely supportive of developments in the Monteverdi Choir and Orchestra. At the launch of the Bach Cantata Pilgrimage in 2000, for example, Prince Charles spoke at a reception at Painters' Hall in London, and displayed not only his knowledge of the music, but his personal enthusiasm for the project that we were about to undertake. It was inspiring to everyone present

– especially those of us who were going to be taking part.

In 2017, Sir John Eliot Gardiner embarked on another ambitious project. In this four hundred and fiftieth anniversary year of Monteverdi's birth he set out to perform all three of his surviving operas – *Orfeo*, *The Return of Ulysses* and *The Coronation of Poppea* – in consecutive performances across Europe and the US. This was hugely expensive and we were immensely grateful for the support from our patron in hosting a concert and fundraising dinner at Buckingham Palace at the beginning of the project. For me, the event is encapsulated in a photo of Prince Charles cracking up in response to one of my (probably awful) jokes in the presence of my wife and Carol Grigor, our longstanding main sponsor. It was a wonderful evening. In the summer, Ann and I were enthralled to hear all three operas performed at La Fenice in Venice. The whole venture was a great success – in no small measure due to Prince Charles's involvement.

Enjoying a joke with Prince Charles, Patron of the Monteverdi Choir at a reception in Buckingham Palace in 2017 as Ann and Carol Grigor, the main sponsor of the Monteverdi organisation, look on.

11. TRAVELLING THE WORLD

One of the rewards of a successful career in academia is the opportunity it affords for travel. Both in my professional capacity and recreationally, I have travelled the globe and learnt a great deal from the experience. Travel is important not just for the adventure itself, but because it enhances ones's understanding and appreciation of other cultures and ways of life. Understanding difference is the route to a civilised society and a starting point to address some of the world's great political conundrums. Reading about other cultures is not enough – you have to experience them at first hand. As with *Desert Island Discs*, I have chosen just eight places to which I have travelled that have special meaning for both my professional and personal life. If I were ever to be cast away on a desert island these are some of the most memorable places to which I would dream of returning.

1: CHINA. I have visited China on several occasions, most recently just two years ago. The University of Edinburgh has developed a shared programme with the Zhejiang University in Haining, just west of Shanghai, which offers joint undergraduate and postgraduate courses. In 2019 I was invited there to spend a week teaching and visiting their hospital. My lectures seemed to be well received but I was challenged on the wards, where – in a way that reminded me very much of my first years in Edinburgh – my hosts lined up some highly complex cancer patients for my advice. One case involved a patient with advanced lung cancer. All conventional treatments had been tried and I was asked what I would now do. The only option, I said, was to try experimental medicines and I explained that I would ask the patient whether or not they wanted to do this. 'Oh, the patient does not know that he has cancer,' came the reply. 'It is up to his family to make such decisions for him.' This approach was so completely different to ours, but important to know about, especially in view of possible future joint research projects.

Shanghai is one of the most exciting cities I have ever visited and I have been there several times. On my first trip, I walked along the Bund, imagining my grandfather's ship lying at anchor there after the long sea voyage from the Bristol Channel. Across the water was wasteland, but now this has been transformed, and the skyline resembles Manhattan with skyscrapers and cranes everywhere. Until recently, Hong Kong was a similarly exciting city and one I have also enjoyed visiting, not just for its landscape but for its food – and the opportunity to get suits made in 48 hours. I remember in particular several interesting work meetings about their hospice movement and attitudes to palliative care.

In 2007 Ann and I undertook the longest and most adventurous of all our expeditions to China. Starting in Xian, the site of the famous terracotta warriors, we travelled 9000 miles west following the ancient Silk Route. Travelling by plane, train, car and even camel, we journeyed through Kyrgyzstan to Uzbekistan. This was challenging for us but the distances and rigours of climate gave us a profound respect for the ancient traders.

2: JAPAN. In 2010 I was invited to Tokyo to discuss the different approaches to licensing medicines between Japan and the West and the challenges this poses for global approval of new drugs. After the meeting, Ann joined me for a brief tour to Kyoto and, via the bullet train, Hiroshima, where we were deeply moved by the memorial to the atomic bomb explosion

3: INDIA. I have visited three times –in 1994, 1999 and 2016 – but would love to go back. My first visit involved lecturing in Mumbai, Bangalore, Mysore, Madras and Delhi, and – apart from a trip to see the Taj Mahal at Agra – hardly any sightseeing at all. These lecture tours can be quite demanding. Often there's an early flight, an afternoon symposium and then a banquet dinner, and although all are enjoyable in their different ways, in hot and humid venues it can be quite energy-sapping. I will, however, always remember Chennai, which I visited when it was still called Madras. After an afternoon symposium in a very humid lecture hall, a young trainee oncologist was assigned to look after me until the evening dinner. He offered to show me a famous local temple, but I opted instead for a walk along the beach to refresh myself before the inevitable gargantuan banquet. Shoes and socks off, we waded in the shallows, watching the locals washing their water buffaloes in the surf. Soon we came across a group of about a dozen young men and women sitting in a circle on the beach, apparently engaged in serious conversation. My host invited me to join them and I found myself listening to an earnest discussion about the meaning of life and what people hoped for in the future. I was quizzed about my own spiritual beliefs and how I had become a doctor and what I myself wanted from life. On leaving, I thanked my host for introducing me to his friends. He replied that he had never met any of them before but it was commonplace for young people to gather in this way at the end of the day to share their thoughts about the most important things in life. I was impressed and deeply moved not just by the openness of this discussion but by their willingness to include a stranger like myself. An encounter that I will never forget.

On subsequent visits to Rajasthan and the south of the country we have been impressed with the friendliness of many people that we have encountered from very different backgrounds. And we saw a tiger – a wonderful beast, much larger than the lions we saw on safari in Africa. I definitely want to go back.

4: SOUTH AMERICA. Edinburgh University's global health programme has established links with many parts of the world. In 2013 I accompanied our principal and our chair of general practice to Santiago in Chile to discuss public health and anticancer strategies. This was a brief trip with no time for sightseeing but I should like to return one day. Chile seemed a most interesting and varied country – and they make excellent wine.

Visiting Peru, Ann and I found Machu Picchu even more inspiring than the travel brochures suggest. On a separate trip to Ecuador we were fascinated by the Galapagos Islands, whose geological and biological diversity is extraordinary and a reminder of the essential need for conservation of the natural world. As with climate change, it is all too easy to say this but leave action to others. I like to remember that Charles Darwin started out as a medical student in Edinburgh before turning to natural history. There is an impressive portrait of the great man in the Athenaeum in London, the club to which I belong. I always nod in appreciation when passing it.

5: EGYPT. In 1993 I paid my only visit to Egypt, visiting Cairo and Aswan, where I had been invited to host a seminar. In Cairo I visited the famous museum which houses the world's largest collection of ancient Egyptian artefacts. Like the Louvre in Paris, you would need days to see just a fraction of the exhibits, but even on this short visit I was humbled to reflect on the brevity of our own lifespans compared to the thousands of years of history on display. Everyone visiting Cairo has to see the pyramids and I duly paid homage. The largest one is five hundred feet high and it is almost impossible to imagine how its two million blocks of stone were cut, transported and assembled 2,500 years before the birth of Christ. Leaving Cairo, I flew down the Nile to Aswan, the site of the world's largest embankment dam. I was fascinated by the Nile and spent an afternoon sailing in one of the traditional red-sailed feluccas. The water was black and silky with an oily appearance I have never seen anywhere else. I should like to return one day and sail its entire length.

6: ROMANIA. As an oncologist, I have always been particularly interested in what we now call palliative care. This includes all aspects of symptom relief but especially focuses on the physical and emotional care of patients nearing the end of life. As I have already mentioned, I served on the governing board of Edinburgh's St Columba's Hospice for many years and created our first chair of palliative medicine in our university. This aspect of medicine epitomises the need for good communication between everyone involved in providing holistic care.. One of the first things that I did on retiring from clinical practice was to write a small book entitled *Communicating with Cancer Patients** to help trainee doctors and nurses. After giving a talk about it, I was invited to go to Romania to help with their development of palliative care. My hosts from the Hospice Casa Sperantei in Brasov, founded by English businessman Graham Perolls in 1992 as part of his Hospices of Hope charity, explained that although hospice care was beginning to be developed in Romania, the concept of palliative care was not so appreciated in its hospitals – indeed there was some resistance from doctors, as there had been in the UK in the 1970s. There was clearly a huge need for education and as a result of this first visit in 2018 I gathered together a few key colleagues in Edinburgh and, along with Graham Perolls, we began to develop a plan for sharing our expertise and experience with our

**Communicating with Cancer Patients by John F. Smyth* (CRC Press, 2014)

Romanian colleagues. Sadly, the Covid pandemic put our plans on hold but I hope that we can return to this important work as soon as possible.

7: VIENNA. For me, no dream destination list would be complete without including this wonderful city. Its history, architecture, surrounding countryside and – above all – music are truly inspiring. I have visited Vienna many times for work but just walking its streets, sitting in its cafes and listening to the ever-present music acts as an always reliable emotional reboot. I want to return there as often as possible.

8: NEW YORK. Another favourite city, a complete contrast to Vienna but in its own way equally exciting. I first visited as a student but have returned countless times for work and for pleasure. The fact that three of those journeys across the Atlantic involved flying on Concorde, that we've been there on family holidays, and that I've sung in the Lincoln Center and Carnegie Hall – all cement New York even more firmly in my affections. Meetings with colleagues in the pharmaceutical industry often took me there and the hard work we did on drug development plans was usually followed by dinner in a wonderful restaurant and being put up in a first-class hotel. Sadly for the present generation, such lavishness is no longer allowed, but at least I have been left with wonderful memories of the Lotte New York Palace on Madison Avenue (almost as good as the awesome Swiss Hotel in Istanbul in my opinion), while the dry martinis at the Waldorf Astoria must surely be the original – and best – 'sharpener'!

So I have recorded here just some of the wonderful places to which I have travelled and met people who have in turn influenced my medical life. Learning how best to help those suffering from serious illness is greatly helped by an appreciation of our diversity and an understanding of what matters most to different cultures, how people differ in their ambitions and – especially for an oncologist – their attitudes to the balance between life and death. My travels have taught me to better understand patients' attitude to life's big challenges such as a diagnosis of cancer. This has been humbling but reinvogorating too.

The Taj Mahal.

The best way to visit the pyramids. Cairo, 1993.

Ann and I on safari in the Masai Mara, Kenya, 1996.

12: EPILOGUE

When I reflect on my life, I realise how very lucky I have been. I was born into a loving family, had an excellent education both at school and at university and, having been uncertain about a career choice between music or medicine, I have been fortunate to enjoy both. Being appointed to a professorship at an early age was a particular challenge, and what began as a department of one grew to have more than two hundred staff when I left thirty years later: by analogy with music, I started out like a pianist giving a solo recital and ended up conducting a large orchestra in a symphony hall. Throughout my career, clinical medicine has always taken priority over research and administration. During my thirty years as a professor, I took care of over 6,000 families affected by cancer, and from them shaped my opinions on priorities in cancer care. The job always involved both taking responsibility for difficult decisions and sharing intimate knowledge of patients' hopes, fears and expectations, and I do miss it.

Considering how little we knew about the biology of tumours, and how few tools we had at our disposal, the progress that has been made in cancer treatment over the past fifty years is astonishing. We now have much greater understanding of how tumours grow, the relationship between the tumour and its host, and can see far more easily if it has spread. It is hard to believe that when I started out in medical oncology we did not have CT scans, let alone MRI or PET imaging.

We now have several hundred drugs for treating cancer, and the whole process of drug development has changed beyond recognition. Two key aspects of this were the brilliant outcomes of the Human Genome Project, which continues to give us insights into new targets for drug development, and the emergence of immunotherapy. I am proud of the part that my team have played in helping to develop more sophisticated ways to test potential new drugs in the laboratory and then refining the way we test them in patients. Teamwork is absolutely essential here, and I was fortunate to gather around me a group of doctors, nurses, scientists, psychologists and data managers to make this research exciting and rewarding – for staff and patients alike. Together we have made a significant contribution to 'taming' the unruliness of cancer.

The European Organisation for Research and Treatment of Cancer (EORTC) took a lead in this and again I take pride in the contribution that I was able to make in creating its Pharmacokinetics and Metabolism Group, in helping develop its Early Clinical Trials group, and my ten years as editor-in-chief of their journal, *The European Journal of Cancer*. My wife Ann led the organisation's Quality of Life Group at a key time when they were developing instruments to record patients' own experience of cancer treatments and these are still used worldwide. This naturally brought significant acclaim to the Edinburgh centre. In 2022 the EORTC celebrates its sixtieth anniversary and I can look back warmly to my contribution spanning forty-six of those.

My mentor Gordon Hamilton Fairley was ahead of his time in believing that the immune system held the key to cancer progression. The treatment approaches in his time aiming to stimulate the immune system in patients with acute myeloid leukaemia were, however, astonishingly crude, and not surprisingly, unsuccessful. Over the past decade we have witnessed the emergence of truly successful immunotherapy, with molecules that can specifically reawaken a sleeping immune system. Not only is this approach successful at destroying cancer cells but, as in the case of polio or diphtheria vaccinations, this gives the patient's immune system 'memory' for potential lifelong protection from tumour recurrence – in other words, a possible cure. I have been fortunate to contribute to this development both through serving as an independent monitor of international clinical trials of new immunotherapeutics and advising several pharmaceutical companies on trial design.

Another significant development over the past fifty years has been the oversight of clinical trials by governments. The UK has played a pivotal role in this by establishing the Committee on Safety of Medicines (CSM) following the thalidomide tragedy in the 1960s. This was created by none other than Sir Eric Scowan, the architect of the ICRF endowment to Edinburgh, and the senior assessor on my appointment committee back in 1978. I served on the committee for many years and am proud of the contribution that I was able to make as its only oncologist at a time when more and more new anticancer drugs were seeking approval. Licensing of new medicines is dependent on weighing the balance between efficacy and safety, and unfortunately in the case of anticancer drugs, this is often marginal. The side-effects of many anticancer medicines are really challenging but as I mentioned earlier, one of the most rewarding research programmes I ever led was the development of a new class of anti-sickness drugs we pioneered in the 1980s. The fact that I was invited to travel the world to report our results was an additional bonus.

I have not written much about teaching in these pages but I have greatly enjoyed passing on my knowledge and experience, particularly to undergraduate students. Ever since arriving in Edinburgh I have been constantly aware of the need to help people understand more about cancer – what it actually is, how it is assessed, how it is managed, and the likely outcomes. There is still an inappropriate fear of the very mention of the word 'cancer' and widespread misunderstanding about the value of different treatment approaches – although in both cases, not nearly as bad as in the 1970s, when the whole subject was taboo. In my early years in Edinburgh I held countless meetings with hospital specialists and GPs to try to explain what was possible and our approach to holistic care. I particularly enjoyed teaching the medical students about this and found their young minds very receptive to new ideas and understanding of the need for sensitive explanations for patients to lessen fear and anxiety.

Modern technology is helping the daily practice of medicine in many ways, but one aspect that is problematic is the introduction of electronic notes. With old-fashioned written patients' notes being replaced by ones on computer, the doctor can spend most of a consultation looking at the screen and not observing the patient's response to their conversation. It is, however, good to reflect that the whole doctor/patient relationship has evolved significantly over the years I was in practice. No longer does the doctor decide what is best for the patient and tell him or her what is going to happen next. The conversation that now takes place between them is so much more appropriate but there are potential pitfalls. Nowadays there are often several choices open to a patient at different times during their experience of cancer. But while it is the doctor's responsibility to explain options and the patient's right to choose, there is a real risk that patients are left to decide on their own, with the doctor devolving too much responsibility for really difficult decisions. Ironically, this situation will only get worse as more and more treatments become available. The best doctor/patient relationship is a partnership. When asking a patient whether or not they would like to participate in a clinical trial, for example, I used the expression of whether they would 'like to join me' in this particular piece of research? Partnership yes, but just as in music, the performer (patient) needs a conductor (doctor) to arrive at a harmonious outcome.

Apart from taxes, death is the only certainty awaiting us all. Perhaps as an oncologist I have been too used to talking about death, but I still find that a lot of doctors are reluctant to discuss it with patients. Learning how to help people face the inevitable is an essential part of practising oncology. Far from being a taboo subject, I have had many very moving conversations with patients and their families in helping them to prepare for death.

One of the most important responsibilities for an oncologist is to know when is the right time to stop active treatment – trying to control the tumour – and focus on palliative care, treating symptoms, both physical and psychological. In my early days, there were so few treatment options available that talking about the hows and whens of death took up much of our conversations. As we have developed more and more treatments, so the hopes of patients are raised both initially and during the roller-coaster experience of remissions and relapses, and the constant possibility of further choices. It is the latter that needs to be managed carefully. On so many occasions, I have realised that the patient has had enough, but the family and closest companions want treatment to continue – anything to keep their loved one alive for as long as possible. In this situation, the doctor shouldn't opt out of the difficult conversation to explain that it is time to stop, and take the easier option of suggesting that there is still something that could be tried. This is where good communication is critical, and I have had many experiences of helping families come to an acceptance, allowing them time to have the essential conversations in private, but without avoiding the 'elephant in the room'.

I particularly remember caring for a delightful retired shepherd who had advanced melanoma in the days before immunotherapy. He only had a few months to live – which I gently explained to him in the presence of his daughter, a nurse. The shepherd lived in a humble cottage by the sea with his companion of sixteen years – his beloved sheepdog. The daughter asked about research trials and I explained that, although this was certainly a possibility, it would mean her father coming to the hospital frequently for monitoring. She said that her father could come and live nearby with her, but it was clear that the shepherd was not keen to do so. Although father and daughter were very close, in a private moment he explained to me that there was no room in his daughter's flat for his dog. He made the right decision. He died a few weeks after this conversation, and shortly afterwards the daughter came to see me. She thanked me for helping them both and reported that during his final days she was able to visit him frequently. Sitting outside his cottage with his dog by his side, she said that they had had some of the most meaningful conversations they had ever shared. He had a good death. Two weeks after the shepherd's death, the dog died also. Grief and bereavement are powerful emotions.

Science is judged by grant funding and publications. With the support of excellent colleagues, I raised over £30 million in research funds and have published over three hundred and thirty papers in scientific journals. I have also written, edited or contributed chapters to forty-two books. Of all the fellowships I have been awarded, as a physician I particularly prize my Fellowship of the Royal College of Surgeons in Edinburgh. This was given in consideration of my contribution to education in a multidisciplinary setting. Above all, I am especially proud of my Fellowship of the Royal Society of Edinburgh, Scotland's National Academy, on whose public engagement committee I currently serve. I have enjoyed my role as an assistant principal in the university for the past twelve years, and I'm still involved in cancer research as chairman of the Cancer Drug Development Forum, which keeps me in touch with academia, the pharmaceutical industry, and the regulators who award licences for useful new medicines.

I still enjoy flying small aeroplanes, and over the past ten years have learnt how to fish for salmon in the Scottish rivers. Contrary to the ribbing I get from friends and family, I do actually catch fish – sometimes! When I was young, my cousin Michael Stear taught me the art of coarse fishing on the Thames. I would happily spend hours watching a little float bob around, then suddenly disappear underwater, to reward me with a small perch. I learnt to love being beside the river, watching wildlife and nature change with the seasons. Now I fish for salmon on the Tay in Perthshire – surely one of the most beautiful rivers in the world. To spend a day wading in the shallows, or fishing from a boat with the local ghillie, casting a fly from a fifteen-foot rod, is an experience that only fishermen understand. It is hard work if you keep at it for seven hours, but wonderful to experience nature all around you: above you, the ever-changing sky, across the river, the trees gently stirring in the breeze; and everywhere wildlife – kingfishers, ospreys, and sometimes fish jumping from the water to tease, and then the thrill of a 'take' and the ensuing few minutes while the fish tries to outwit you. It's a magnificent sport. We used to be allowed to bring the occasional fish home to the smokie , but now, for conservation, we return them all to grow even larger.

As the years go by, friends – and especially family – have become ever more important. The greatest good fortune of all is to love and be loved by my two daughters, my two stepdaughters, and most especially, my wife Ann. I have written of the enjoyment that both of us find in our ten grandchildren, and have compiled this reflection of some of the most important parts of my life partly with them in mind. Family history is important. I look forward hopefully to living for as long as possible, to seeing these intelligent, lively, and curious young people grow up and take their place in what for now, seems to be a very challenging world. But perhaps it has always been?

With my cousin Michael Stear in 2009

Receiving the fellowship of the Royal College of Surgeons, Edinburgh from the President Prof PS Boulter, in 1994

A beautiful salmon caught on the Tay and returned to grow even larger.

ACKNOWLEDGEMENTS

In the pages of this memoir I have tried to acknowledge many of the people who have had the greatest influence on my life. I am immensely grateful to all of them – parents, teachers, mentors, colleagues, many of the thousands of patients for whom it was my privilege to be responsible and, above all, my family. All have shaped me in so many ways. Here I want to thank particularly those people who have helped me to make this book a reality.

My personal assistant, Lisa Wood, has been organising my busy life and deciphering my handwriting with astonishing patience for over twenty years. She typed the first draft and has played a key role in this particular project. So too did David Robinson, whose skill as an editor has been enormously helpful throughout. I am also grateful to Abigail Salvesen for skill in designing the book, and especially to Alexander McCall Smith for his encouragement and support.

My daughters, step-daughters and their delightful families were a starting point for these reflections, and I hope they find the end result interesting. Most of all, I thank my wife Ann for her many suggestions while editing the first draft, but most of all for her love and enduring support over the years. I dedicate this memoir to her.

ABBREVIATIONS

ADA – Adenosine Deaminase
CHM – Commission on Human Medicines
CRC – Cancer Research Campaign
CSM – Committee on the Safety of Medicines
DCF – deoxycoformycin
EORTC – European Organisation for Research and
                 Treatment of Cancer
ESMO – European Society of Medical Oncology
MHRA – Medical and Healthcare products
                 Regulatory Authority
MRC – Medical Research Council
MRCP – Member of the Royal College of Physicians
ICRF – Imperial Cancer Research Fund
NCI – National Cancer Institute (US)
NIH – National Institutes of Health (US)